Rosanne *Saylofsky*

Best wishes and
thanks for your
leadership —
Dale Parnell

LogoLearning™

Dale Parnell

LogoLearning™

Searching for Meaning in Education

CENTER FOR OCCUPATIONAL RESEARCH AND DEVELOPMENT

Reproduction or translation of any part of this work beyond that permitted
by Sections 107 and 108 of the 1976 United States Copyright Act without the
permission of the copyright owner is unlawful. Requests for permission or
further information should be addressed to
    Permissions Department
    CORD Communications
    P.O. Box 21206
    Waco, Texas 76702-1206

LogoLearning is a trademark and service mark of Dale Paul Parnell
Book Design by Kenneth Turbeville
Grateful acknowledgement is made to Anne Christian Buchanan for her editorial
work to this book as well as Jennifer Jackson and Julie Vitale for their role in the
research and development of the book.

ISBN 1-55502-519-6
Library of Congress Number 94-070282

Printed in the United States of America

Dedication

To the host of dedicated and hard-working

classroom instructors and educational administrators

who keep our schools and colleges operating,

sometimes against great odds.

I tip my hat in appreciation to you.

Table of Contents

Foreword

Few writers can speak from the breadth of experience and depth of knowledge about education issues that Professor Dale Parnell brings to this book. He has served as a high school teacher, a principal, a school superintendent, a state superintendent of public instruction, a college president, the president and chief executive officer of the American Association of Community and Junior Colleges, and now a university professor. He has also had a long love affair with classroom instruction. All of this interest and experience gives Dale Parnell a unique vantage point from which to view America's educational systems. It is clear that this book has been written from the heart as well as from the head.

American education has undergone intense scrutiny and critical appraisal in the past decades. If reports and studies alone could develop quality in education, excellence would have been achieved long ago. Most of the recommendations are familiar: more accountability, school choice, national standards, more tests, longer school years, site-based management. However, few of these reports have given much attention to the question of what happens when the instructor closes the classroom door. In this valuable, new book Dale Parnell clearly shines the spotlight upon teaching and learning.

His book, *The Neglected Majority,* was chosen the best national association book in 1985 and quickly became a classic in education literature. In that book Parnell advocated the development of a Tech Prep/Associate Degree applied-learning program for secondary and postsecondary students. Commencing with the eleventh grade in high school and concluding with the associate degree in a community, technical, or junior college, the tech-prep program is aimed at serving that host of students not likely to earn a four-year college baccalaureate degree. This revolutionary course of study has now gone from an original idea to a congressionally funded program that is being implemented in schools and colleges all across the country.

This book is a natural follow-on to *The Neglected Majority* and will, over time, become another classic in education literature. Parnell outlines a commonsense but ever-so-important strategy for improving teaching and learning. It is important for giving the tech-prep program a solid philosophical and pedagogical base.

It is a pleasure to recommend this book to anyone interested in education, particularly classroom teachers. I predict it will be an important addition to the library of anyone involved in teacher education and should be studied by anyone planning to become a teacher at any level of education.

Kinsey B. Green
Dean, College of Home Economics and Education
Oregon State University
Corvallis, Oregon

LogoLearning

The "Four $\mathcal{A}$s" of Meaningful Education

- *Learning for Acquisition of Knowledge.* Students acquire information and retain it sufficiently to apply it toward or associate it with some real-life situation.

- *Learning for Application.* Students are actively engaged in practicing and processing what they learn within the context of varied real-life situations, performing authentic tasks to gain an understanding of how the information applies in everyday life.

- *Learning for Assimilation.* Students demonstrate sufficient understanding of the content and context of what they are learning to apply knowledge and skills effectively to new situations.

- *Learning for Association.* The educational experience is organized around problems and themes rather than subject-matter disciplines; students learn to transfer acquisition, application, and assimilation of knowledge to new problem-solving situations.

CHAPTER 1

Keeping Hope Alive

The Case for LogoLearning

The striving to find a meaning in one's life is the primary motivational force in humankind.

–Viktor Frankl

Why do I have to learn this?"

"Because you might need it someday."

That familiar teacher reply has always felt unsatisfying to students. In today's diverse and challenging educational environment it is a woefully inadequate—if all too common—response. Not only does it represent an approach to education that is failing to reach the vast majority of our students, it also ignores the preponderance of recent research into how the brain processes knowledge and how human beings learn most effectively.

What's the alternative? Many promising solutions have been suggested over the past few decades, along with countless strategies for revamping America's schools. But my years of experience as an educator, an administrator, and an advocate for educational reform lead me to suggest *LogoLearning* as the best framework for providing a more effective, satisfying education for all students.

What is LogoLearning? It comes from *logos,* a wonderful Greek word that denotes "meaning." It arises from the early Greek philosophical foundations of meaning, reason, and purpose. The term *LogoLearning,* which marks an educational philosophy and an educational strategy that centers on enabling students to find *meaningfulness* in their education.

In LogoLearning it is the major task of the teacher to broaden the student's perceptions so that meaning becomes visible and the purpose of learning immediately understandable. It is not enough to help students see the specific objectives of a lesson or even of an overall course. Instead, teachers must help students understand the larger meaning of a particular study—how it relates to real-life issues and actual life roles. I am convinced that few educational strategies will so effectively help individuals learn as understanding the connection between classroom subject matter and the problems and challenges they will encounter in the course of their lives.

The LogoLearning approach to education borrows deliberately from the work of Viktor Frankl, who founded the psychological practice called logotherapy. Frankl forged his understanding of the importance of meaning to the human experience in the crucible of a Nazi concentration camp. His bestselling and influential book, *Man's Search for Meaning: An Introduction to Logotherapy*, proclaims, "There is nothing in the world... that would so effectively help one to survive even the worst conditions, as the knowledge that there is meaning in one's life."[1]

As a prisoner of the Nazis, forced to endure bestial conditions and to watch countless fellow prisoners die, Frankl observed that a sense of meaning and purpose is a crucial component—perhaps the crucial component—in human survival. Prisoners who had a "why" or a purpose for living were the ones who could best bear the horrible "how" of their daily living. A loss of hope and meaning was all too often the fatal blow to Frankl's fellow prisoners:

> The death rate in the week between Christmas 1944, and New Year's 1945, increased in camp beyond all previous experience.... The explanation for this increase did not lie in the harder working conditions, or the deterioration of our food supplies, or a change of weather, or new epidemics. It was simply that the majority of the prisoners had lived in the naïve hope that they would be home again by Christmas. As the time drew near and there was no encouraging news, the prisoners lost courage and disappointment overcame them. This had a dangerous influence on their powers of resistance, and a great number of them simply died.[2]

Frankl stresses that striving to find some concrete meaning or purpose in one's personal existence provides a primary motivational force for living. And I am convinced that this principle applies to learning as well—that connecting the "why" of concrete reality to the educational process provides an essential motivational force for learning. If students are to be motivated to learn, they must see and feel the touchstone of reality and meaning in their educational experiences.

This idea is not new, of course. As I will explain later in this chapter, LogoLearning draws upon an impressive legacy of thought and practice through the ages and throughout the twentieth century. The best teachers of any time have always taught for meaning, whether as a conscious effort or simply from instinct.

But even the most cursory look at the majority of America's schools shows that large numbers of students are *not* finding meaning in their school experience. They are *not* learning to solve real-life problems or to function as effective members of society. They are not even acquiring the content they are told they will need "someday."

Few things are more dehumanizing, more certain to generate difficulties, than for students to see their education as a meaningless experience. Yet, too often in schools and colleges we allow just that to happen—particularly for that neglected majority of students who are unlikely ever to earn a college baccalaureate degree. When meaning and purpose are lost, hope is lost, and the student is soon lost as well.

The national African American leader Jesse Jackson has it right when he exclaims in his speeches "Keep hope alive!" It is the goal of this book to keep hope alive in education by keeping meaning alive in the educational process.

TAKING EDUCATION OUT OF THE FREEZER

In many of today's classrooms, especially secondary-school classrooms, teaching is a matter of putting students in classrooms marked "English," "history," "math," or so forth and then attempting to fill their heads with facts through lecture, textbooks, and the like. Aside from an occasional lab, workbook, or "story problem," the element of hands-on, active experience is absent, and little attempt is made to connect what students are learning with the world in which they will be expected to spend their lives. Often the fragmented information offered to students is of little use or application except to pass a test.

What we do, in essence is to require students to commit isolated bits of knowledge to memory in isolation from any practical application—to simply take our word that they "might need it someday." This might well be called the freezer approach to teaching and learning. In effect, we are handing out information to our students and saying, "Just put this into your mental freezer; you can thaw it out later should you need it." And with the exception of a minority of academically talented students, students just aren't buying that offer. The majority of students fail to see any meaning in what they are asked to learn—and they just don't learn it.

I recently had occasion to interview seventy-five high school students representing seven different high schools in the Northwest. In nearly all cases the students were high school juniors and identified as average students. Their comments (which I have paraphrased in some cases) illustrate clearly that many of our methods of teaching simply are not getting through to many students:

- "The lecture classes don't keep my attention. I like my home ec. and business classes much better than classes where you just sit and listen."

- "English classes really are boring.... I don't see how I can use most of that stuff. It doesn't mean much to me!"
- "I go to school just for athletics..... Most of my academic classes are so boring I do just enough to stay eligible."
- "I know it is up to me to get a degree, but a lot of times school is just so dull and boring.... You go to this class, go to that class, study a little of this and a little of that, and nothing connects."

One high school student interviewed, summed up our contemporary education problem by exclaiming, "I would like to learn to really understand and know the meaning of something."

The anecdotal evidence provided by these interviews—that traditional classes taught by traditional methods are simply failing to connect with many students—is supported by the results of countless surveys and studies that document the failure of American schools to teach adequate skills. Recent National Assessment of Educational Progress (NAEP) test results, for example, reveal that many of our young people lack the basic skills they need to function successfully in thousands of jobs today:

> Sixty-one percent of 17-year-old students could not read or understand relatively uncomplicated material, such as that typically presented at the high school level. Nearly one-half appeared to have limited mathematics skills and abilities that go little beyond adding, subtracting, and multiplying with whole numbers. More than one-half could not evaluate the procedures or results of a scientific study, and few included enough information in their written pieces to communicate their ideas effectively.[3]

My own experience as a community college president confirms this analysis. In most community colleges today, one-third to one-half of the entering students are enrolled in developmental (remedial) education, trying to make up for what they did not learn in high school.

Clearly, something must change. Arthur Applebee, Judith Langen, and Ina V. S. Mullis point in the right direction—the LogoLearning direction—when they say,

> For qualitatively different gains to occur, the goals of instruction need to be reconsidered. Teaching decisions were once guided by a hierarchy suggesting that students must first learn the facts and skills and later learn to apply them. Yet many educators now recognize the limitations of this stepping-stone view of education. Educational theory and research suggest a different pattern of

generative teaching and learning, where learning content and procedures and how to use this learning for specific purposes occur interactively.... When students engage in activities that require them to use new learning, both their knowledge of content and skills and their ability to use them develop productively together."[4]

As Theodore Sizer[5] and several other leaders have urged, excellence in education will happen only as we deepen student understanding by teaching for meaning. I believe this will require a careful review of educational purposes, time schedules, school organizations, and curricular priorities that work against teaching for meaning.

SEVEN PRINCIPLES THAT CAN TRANSFORM THE CLASSROOM

What is the alternative to "freezer" teaching? What would a meaning-based education look like? There are many possible answers to that good question, and many specific answers have been proposed over the years. Most of these, however, can be distilled into a set of principles that form the framework of the LogoLearning strategy. The application of these principles to instructional development can facilitate learning in the classroom and help students transfer that learning to real-life settings outside the classroom. (These common-sense principles would also be good guidelines for textbook publishers to follow in developing curricula.)

1. *The Purpose Principle:* Teachers help students understand the purpose of any study unit, not only *what* they should learn, but *why*!
2. *The Building Principle:* New knowledge and new units of study are deliberately and specifically connected with students' prior knowledge or past learning so that the new learning builds on prior experience.
3. *The Application Principle:* New knowledge is specifically related to its practical, real-life application—especially how it relates to students' future roles as citizens, consumers, workers, family members, lifelong learners, healthy individuals, and participants in cultural and leisure activities.
4. *The Problem-Solving Principle:* Students are encouraged to become active (rather than passive) learners by using new knowledge and skills to solve problems.
5. *The Teamwork Principle:* Students learn teamwork and cooperation by working together to solve problems. .
6. *The Discovery Principle:* The classroom slogan is "try it!" Students are guided toward *discovering* new knowledge rather

than having the answers (or multiple answers, as is often the case) handed to them. Teachers help students explore, test, and seek their own answers, often with the help of learning partners.

7. *The Connection Principle*: Teachers help students see the connections between context and content, knowledge and application, one discipline and another. Divisions between traditional disciplines are minimized.

SEVEN PRINCIPLES THAT CAN TRANSFORM THE CLASSROOM

1. Purpose
2. Building
3. Application
4. Problem-Solving
5. Teamwork
6. Discovery
7. Connection

What happens when educators shape their instruction around these seven principles? The educational process is transformed, beginning with the attitudes of the students. I saw this clearly in my interviews with high school juniors. When asked about their practically oriented "applied" classes, they responded with unmistakable enthusiasm:

- "I am always doing things in my electronics class. . . . I don't get bored in that class."
- "I love my ag [agriculture] classes, particularly the FFA [Future Farmers of America] activities. . . . I wish my other classes were as interesting."
- "A lot of kids are turned off and tuned out in this school" . . . but that isn't true in my Principles of Technology class (applied physics). . . . The teacher there really tries to help us solve problems. . . . I am beginning to really like science."
- "I like my graphic [arts] classes. . . . I learn more about good communication there than I do in English classes."

I am fully convinced that the perceived differences between these classes and the ones that were written off as "boring" lie not in what is being taught, but in how the teaching is approached. It is the activity-centered but business-like environment in the "applied" classes that accounts for student enthusiasm, and that same environment could be adapted to teach math, English, science, social studies, or any number of traditional subjects.

When students are able to grasp the clear application of the content to real-life situations, they can clearly see the "why" in what they are learning, and thus they are motivated to learn. In the more passively structured, "they talk and you listen," "learn this and you'll use it someday" approach of the more traditional disciplines, they are simply not getting the message. LogoLearning is dedicated to transforming students' educational experience by helping them get the message.

TABLE 1
LOGOLEARNING IN SUMMARY

LOGOLEARNING IS...	LOGOLEARNING IS NOT...
… a relentless search for meaning in the teaching-learning process	… just another gimmick in education flying under a new name
… an avenue to education reform with emphis upon the integration of content with context	… emphasis only upon knowing or only upon doing
… an emphasis upon continuity in	… an unconnected series of school or learning college courses
… a way of helping every student experience success in learning	… a tracking system that separates the "dumb" students from the "smart" ones
… a means of helping students learn to use resources, information, technology, and systems and to work as effective team members	… a system in which students work alone with little understanding of how their learning connects with real-world applications

One simple example of the dynamic way that LogoLearning principles can transform a classroom comes from Doug Dickston, an instructor of English at Mt. Hood Community College in Oregon. Dickston assigns each of his English Composition students a pen pal in another English Comp class. Each week the students write letters to their pen pals, whom they have never met, and Dickston acts as postman to deliver the letters.

The pen-pal strategy gives students an invaluable exposure to real-life communication problems and solutions. A student trying to decipher a confusing comment from a pen pal gains a new appreciation for clear and precise language, and the instructor has a wonderful teaching opportunity as he helps the student pose clear questions to resolve the confusion. Dickston reports that his students often work much harder to make their writing clear to their pen pals than they do in writing essays or other standard class work.

Most of the pen-pal letters hold great interest for their recipients because they are candid and open and based on real events. Older and younger students, males and females, and students from different racial or ethnic backgrounds experience the pleasure of coming to understand one another better while acquiring valuable communication skills. And the students also experience pleasure in the actual process of learning to write more effectively. Pen-pal letters frequently make specific reference to what the students are learning about writing: "Mr. Dickston would not appreciate my using the word *things* here" or "I was surprised to learn using a semicolon is not all that difficult" or "That last sentence I wrote seems like it might be a run-on."

As Doug Dickston is discovering, the benefits of this kind of assignment are many. It introduces a real audience into the communication process. It encourages self-discovery, tolerance, and diplomacy, and it also helps the instructor know the students better. It serves as a barometer of students' progress. Most important, it enables the instructor to inject meaning into the classroom without using up more instruction time.[6]

Yet another example of LogoLearning's capacity to transform education comes from a very different source. Edwin M. Bridges, a professor at Stanford University, has done considerable teaching and research on an instructional strategy called Problem Based Learning (PBL), which makes solving problems the primary focus of the teaching process. In reviewing the outcome of problem-based programs used in training physicians, Bridges concludes that "compared with traditional programs in medical education, PBL yields superior or equivalent results on all but one of the outcome measured studies."[7]

What is striking, in terms of LogoLearning, is that medical students experiencing PBL teaching methods tend toward a meaning orientation. In other words, instead of focusing on memorization (a primary aspect of most medical education), they strive to understand the application of the knowledge. Researchers in medical education, such as John Bransford, indicate that medical students who experience teaching within the context of application are much more likely to transfer that information to solve new problems than are students taught in traditional fact-oriented ways.[8]

TABLE 2
PROBLEM-BASED LEARNING IN MEDICAL EDUCATION: SUMMARY OF RESEARCH

OUTCOMES STUDIED	RESULTS
Attitudes toward the instructional environment	PBL substantially more positive
Approaches to studying	PBL students adopt meaning orientation (desirable outcome); traditional students adopt reproducing orientation

Career preferences	PBL students more likely become primary physicians (desirable); traditional lecture-oriented students become specialists
Completion time and rates	PBL students complete in less time and at a higher rate than traditional students
Knowledge of basic disciplines	Small differences favor traditional lecture-based programs, but PBL students show steeper growth during period of study
Clinical competence	Small differences favor students in PBL programs
Study loads	No major differences

BUT WHAT ABOUT CONTENT?

LogoLearning represents new possibilities and new hope for countless students who would otherwise remain on the educational margins. It means an exciting connection between what goes on in schools and what goes on in the real world.

What it does *not* mean is that students will graduate from high school or college without being able to multiply 8 times 9 or to know the content of the Bill of Rights. It does not mean that students will go through school without being able to read, write, or compute. It doesn't even necessarily mean that students will embark on their future careers without knowing the capital of Illinois (although they *will* have a much better understanding of *why* it became the capital).

The fact that LogoLearning emphasizes meaning, context, and application, does not mean that it neglects content. Rather, it stresses that without context, content is often lost. Teaching for knowledge *cannot be separated* from teaching for meaning—from helping students understand the purpose of what they are asked to do in the classroom. The majority of learners simply do not put knowledge in their mental "deep freezers" unless they can see a real purpose for doing so. And by far the best way to help students understand that purpose is to provide them with hands-on, concrete experience that relates directly to the roles they will play in life.

Unfortunately, an understanding of this simple, transforming reality is often lost in the historical battle between those who stress knowledge in education and those who stress application. Some of the most exciting innovations in education are founded upon the rocks of hard-line arguments between "content" advocates and "context" supporters.

Those on the knowledge-content bandwagon have accused the learn-by-doing advocates of academic anemia. ("They need to know facts, not just a bunch of vague ideas." "Students don't know what's good for them; it's insane to let them learn only what they think is interesting." "School is more than just job training; students need a solid academic foundation!")

And those on the learn-by-doing side, many of them vocational teachers, have often lost touch with the fact that students do need a certain body of knowledge and academic abilities to function and succeed in their culture. ("What's the point of having them learn Shakespeare or sociology; it won't help them get a job!" "You don't really need to understand all that math to make it in the real world.")

LogoLearning insists that these two positions can and must find common ground. Quality education does not mean making a choice between academic rigor (knowledge) on one side or contextual learning (application) on the other side. It's time to question the assumptions underlying these forced dichotomies and to focus instead on how application can bolster knowledge and knowledge can make application meaningful. This kind of synergy and connectedness is precisely what LogoLearning offers.

Let no one misinterpret the basic tenet of LogoLearning—that content is equally important with context, but that context may well determine whether or not the content is actually learned. The two functions of education are obvious: knowing and doing. Both are essential, and the two are inextricably linked. Knowledge that is simply poured, as by funnel, into the human mind, that in no way modifies behavior or creates a reaction or causes an expression, is likely knowledge gone to waste.

One can only wonder where in the history of teaching and learning we have lost an emphasis upon the action part of the process. A young child handles things, explores, sets up, knocks down, puts together, pulls apart, creeps, walks, climbs, talks, imitates, and draws. Yet in the schooling process, particularly in the upper grades and in college the primary emphasis is on the passive learning processes of looking, listening, and memorizing. How can the teaching-learning process keep alive our native tendencies toward action, toward applying knowledge and finding out what it means?

Whatever else we are as human beings, we have an innate desire for meaning. The need to find meaning is a strong motivational force in the life of each of us. If teachers can consistently help students connect subject matter content with the context of application, I believe we will be astonished with the significant increase in learning.

It is the highest form of irony for students to be unable to connect their real-life experiences with schooling or to apply their schooling experiences to real life. When we deny an individual the touchstone of reality, we have effectively reduced the possibility for analytical thinking and understanding. Knowledge may be there in the form of random facts, but knowledge acquires meaning only when it sheds light upon purposes, judgments, and experiences.

Have we gotten so far away from the practical in an education stuffed with abstractions and glib verbosities that we have grown blind to the profound and practical issues of life? LogoLearning sets out to reverse that trend, to build information that is full of meaning and understanding that is grounded in the fertile soil of concrete experience.

THE LOGOLEARNING LEGACY

There really is no education worthy of the name *new*, and as we have seen, LogoLearning is no exception. Great teachers throughout history have placed heavy emphasis on the search for meaning, have motivated their students by relating ideas and knowledge with the practical realities of daily life, and have encouraged them to learn through hands-on, practical experience. I would even venture to say, because LogoLearning is so deeply rooted in the way the human mind is designed to work, that wherever substantial learning has taken place, LogoLearning principles have been at work.

More specifically, however, LogoLearning has its roots in nineteenth- and early twentieth-century educational psychology and philosophy. Wilhelm Wundt (1832–1920), one of the founders of modern psychology, advocated an integration of knowledge with experience and cognition with activity. But it was the work of the physician, psychologist, and philosopher William James

(1842–1910) that gave to LogoLearning its most fertile resources for growth. It might be argued, in fact, that the growth of the educational philosophy that now fully blossoms into LogoLearning has been fed from the deep taproots of James's thought.

William James: The Historical Father of LogoLearning

"No reception without reaction, no impression without correlative expression" was the rule that James espoused for teachers.[9] Because he believed that the human mind played an active role in organizing thought and that the perception of truth is rooted in experience, James urged teachers to help their pupils put new knowledge to immediate use—to help them build up useful systems of association that combined knowing with doing.

The key to James's influence lies in his clarity of vision and the persuasiveness of his writing. Many of James's works influenced educators, including *Talks to Teachers on Psychology* (1892), *Pragmatism* (1907), *A Pluralistic Universe* (1909), and *The Meaning of Truth* (1909), but *Principles of Psychology*, published in 1880, is clearly his most enduring educational legacy. (John Dewey once said that *Principles* was the book that most influenced his thinking.)

James was a shaper and a proponent of functional psychology, which concerns itself with how the conscious mind works. He contended that the mind operates in an active, purposeful way to organize thought and to process experience. James was also a leader in the pragmatist movement of philosophy. As a pragmatist, he held that truth emerges from human experience rather than existing independent of experience, and that beliefs and knowledge cannot be separated from action and experience.

As a result of both these emphases (functionalism and pragmatism), the cognitive process of connecting knowing and doing was central to James' theory of teaching. At the same time, he was wary of an unbalanced approach that sacrificed actual content in the interest of "making learning interesting." In *Talks to Teachers* he expressed the fear that education was growing too soft and permissive: "Soft pedagogies have taken the place of the old steep and rocky path to learning. From this lukewarm air the bracing oxygen of effort is left out. It is nonsense to suppose that every step in education can be interesting."[10]

The Rise of Behaviorism

For a few decades following James' first works, his influence on education was eclipsed (and in some educational circles is still eclipsed) by behaviorism, a psychological approach which concentrates on observable behavior rather than the conscious working of the mind. Led by Edward Lee Thorndike (1874–1949), the first behaviorists decided that what went on in the mind was not externally observable and was therefore not an appropriate object of study, but *behavior* could be observed and quantified. (For example, you cannot objectively measure how and what a dog thinks about its food, but you can measure the food in a dish and how fast the dog is running toward the dish.) Instead of worrying about how organisms thought, therefore, behaviorists concerned themselves with observing how they behaved in response to certain stimuli. In the earlier forms of behaviorism the effort was made to quantify the stimulus (S) and the response (R) to that stimulus and thereby to arrive at an empirical science of measurable *behavioral units*.[11]

Educators who followed the behaviorist approach accordingly would prescribe the stimulus (teaching methods) and observe the response (student behavior) or would attempt to change the behavior by altering the stimulus, but they did not worry much about the thinking process that connected the two—the connection which might be called the "cognitive hyphen" (S-R) between stimulus and response.

Granted, this is a simplistic description of behaviorist psychology and behaviorist educational theory, but for the first two or three decades of the twentieth century such a description would not be far off the mark. And behaviorism has maintained a powerful influence on both psychological and educational thought. In fact, it was not until the 1930s and 1940s that certain psychologists began to concentrate once again on the "hyphen" between S-R and the larger "whole" of the thinking process.

A group of psychologists known collectively as Gestaltists were among the first to do this. Max Wertheimer, the founder of the Gestalt philosophy, did some important work in the area of cognition, but it was Kurt Lewin who brought Gestalt psychology to the forefront of American education. Lewin challenged S-R psychology as being incomplete and endeavored to marry behaviorism with the cognitive elements of perception, learning, and problem-solving.

Dewey's Misunderstood Legacy

As a philosopher, educator, and psychologist, John Dewey (1859–1952) cast a giant shadow on American education in the first half of the twentieth century, especially on the educational reforms of the 1920s, 1930s, and 1940s. Dewey has often been misunderstood, and his ideas, which were complex and sometimes difficult to understand, were sometimes carried to extremes by his followers. Nevertheless, Dewey's influence has been important in the development of LogoLearning.

Like William James, whose work he admired, Dewey was a pragmatist, convinced that truth was grounded in and shaped by experience. But while James primarily emphasized the individual goals for education, Dewey put more stress on the social goals. Dewey developed the "whole child" approach to education, with emphasis upon actual problems of social life and social activity.

Dewey wanted teachers to make use of social settings in the teaching-learning process. He argued repeatedly against confining knowledge and experience into separate domains, insisting that education is not a mere preparation for life, but the process of life itself. He urged that school should not be just a place where students were sent to memorize facts, but also a place where they could practice living in a social context.

These beliefs led Dewey to become a social reconstructionist. He was greatly concerned about social action and change and how individuals relate to society as a whole. He believed that learning involves the modification of behavior in social settings with self-realization as the goal.

The term most commonly used to describe the teaching-learning process Dewey espoused is "life-adjustment education." As he put it, "Human nature exists and operates in an environment, and it is not `in' that environment as coins are in a box, but as a plant is in the sunlight and soil.[12]

John Dewey's work provided the intellectual foundations of the Progressive Education Movement, a term collectively applied to most American education reforms of the 1920s, 1930s, and 1940s. These reforms stressed the theory of learning by doing and influenced such diverse educational initiatives as student government, vocational education, and Head Start.

As is true in so many movements, however, adherents pushed their concepts to extremes. In some educational settings, so much emphasis was placed upon activity that knowledge was nearly overlooked; some "Progressive" classrooms gave short shrift to basic literacy and numeracy skills, reduced the idea of applied knowledge to a narrow utilitarianism, or neglected discipline to the point that some classrooms became chaotic. The Progressive Education movement came to an end with the demise of the Progressive Education Association in 1955.

Unfortunately, its demise is still cited by those who distrust application-centered learning methods. It is a mistake, however, to charge Dewey with the excesses of those who were inspired by his ideas. In many ways Dewey was a strong advocate for a liberal-arts education, with the artistic and aesthetic viewed as the highest levels of experiencing nature. And although he stressed activity and learning by doing, he never advocated the neglect of basic skills or of discipline in the classroom.

It would be a far more serious mistake, however, to allow the excesses of some advocates of Progressive Education to taint the very important ideas Dewey brought to education. There is both a place and a desperate need in today's educational circles for his influence to combine with the concept of application.

We have been struggling for many years endeavoring to get it right in education. In 1931 John Dewey commented in a Harvard lecture:

> We are in the midst of great educational uncertainty, one probably unparalleled at any past time. . . . Conservatives who

urge a return to former standards and practices, and radicals who criticize present conditions agree at least on one point: neither party is satisfied with things the way they are.[13]

It does not appear that much has changed over the past sixty years, for we continue to struggle on into the 1990s!

THE RISE OF COGNITIVE SCIENCE

The 1950s and the 1960s saw the emergence of yet another important line of study that has shaped LogoLearning. This was the study of cognition, or how the mind works in perceiving, remembering, reasoning, and problem solving. Originating in the field of psychology, this realm of endeavor has expanded to include many other disciplines, including education, psychology, linguistics, philosophy, neurology, anthropology, computer science, artificial intelligence, art, music, and mathematics. It has thus come to be known under the more inclusive name of *cognitive science*. The findings of its practitioners about how the mind works and how learners learn have profoundly shaped the concept of LogoLearning.

COGNITIVE SCIENCE: SOME DEFINITIONS

Cognition: The overall functioning of all our mental abilities (such as perceiving, remembering, reasoning, and problem solving).

Cognitive Psychology: The study of knowledge and how people use it.

Cognitive Science: A field of scientific inquiry about knowing and thinking that draws knowledge from many specific disciplines and continues to develop and evolve.

Piaget and the Development of Intelligence

An early contributor to the field of cognitive science, especially as it applies to education, was the Swiss psychologist Jean Piaget (1896–1980). Piaget's early training was in biology, where he developed his interest in the human maturation process. Piaget took his training as a natural scientist into schools, playgrounds, nurseries, and even his own home, interviewing many thousands of children to arrive at a theory of not only what constitutes intelligence, but how a child's intelligence normally develops with age.

As a result of his research with young children, Piaget developed his theory that there are four stages in the cognitive development of children: *sensorimotor* (birth to two years), where the child can only perceive and act upon concrete objects; *preoperational* (two to six years), where the child begins using symbolic and representational thinking and language begins; *concrete operational* (six to twelve years), where the child begins to see logical progressions and can do linear thinking such as in mathematics; and *formal operational* (about age twelve and beyond), where logical deductive thinking begins and acquisition of knowledge begins to be related to experiences. Piaget's studies with young children led him to believe that intelligence is shaped by experience and that action is the key to mental development.

Piaget's research did not receive wide recognition in the United States until the mid-1960s. This recognition was due in some degree to the parallel work of Harvard University's Jerome Bruner, who bridged philosophical and biological theories and thus formed the beginnings of cognitive science. Along with such individuals as Edward Tolman, James Gibson, and Noam Chomsky, Jerome Bruner was responsible for establishing cognitive science as a recognized discipline.

Bruner and the Birth of Cognitive Science

Bruner, who taught and researched at Harvard for twenty-seven years, was greatly influenced by the theories of William James, including his ideas about how the mind organizes experience and his emphasis on experience-based learning. It was Jerome Bruner's work that sparked the renewed interest in understanding the human mind and how best to enhance learning that created a new approach to the study of teaching and learning called cognitive science. His motivation was not to reform behaviorism but to replace it. This philosophy was based upon his belief, after years of research, that understanding and meaning must be the foundation for learning and that the thinking *process* must be emphasized over the stimulus and response philosophy of the behaviorists.

In 1956 Bruner and colleagues published *A Study of Thinking*,[14] which brought the study of cognition new respect in the scientific arena. Bruner developed the theory of concept attainment, which posits that concepts are formed by actively testing hypotheses rather than by repeatedly pairing stimuli and responses. His studies on the science of the mind motivated other researchers to pursue studies on the thinking process.

In addition to his studies of cognition, Bruner shared Piaget's interest in how people learn. His theory of representational systems, spelled out in *Toward a Theory of Instruction*,[15] specified three stages of development that correspond roughly to Piaget's four levels. Typically, in Bruner's construct, the development of intellectual abilities flows from the *inactive* stage, where objects or people are defined by the actions they evoke, to the *iconic* level, where representations exist apart from actions and individuals acquire visual memories, to the *symbolic* stage, where individuals acquire such kinds of knowledge as a verbal symbol system.

Bruner believed that these three stages of intellectual development can be repeated at any age, whenever new information is being processed, and that connections must be made between the three. He also held that learning is enhanced if learners are provided with instruction that is geared to the particular level of intellectual development. Learners at the *iconic* level, for example, should be provided with concrete experiences that allow for the acquisition of new knowledge by relating it to previous experiences.

In *Toward a Theory of Instruction,* Bruner suggests an approach to teaching that is based on an understanding of how what one wishes to teach can best be learned. Bruner suggests four common-sense but vital steps, all of which apply to the LogoLearning construct:

1. Specify the experiences that most effectively implant in the individual a desire for learning (predisposition).
2. Specify how a body of knowledge should be structured so that it can best be learned (structure).
3. Specify the most effective sequence in which to present the knowledge (sequence).
4. Specify the nature and pacing of the learning rewards and punishments aimed at helping the learner grasp, transform, and transfer the learning (reinforcement).

In 1960 Bruner and a colleague, George Miller, established the Center for Cognitive Studies, focusing the study of psychology upon what people *do* as well as upon what they *know.* Their investigations, along with developments in computer technology, have set a contemporary pace for the study of cognitive science in nearly every university in the country.

Cognitive Science and Learning

Even though now four decades old, the field of cognitive science is still developing and encompasses many areas of study. Whereas the study of "thought," or the thinking process, has historically been the special interest of philosophers, cognitive science embraces a wider realm. In fact, one of its key characteristics is that truly it can be called interdisciplinary (see figure 2).

A second characteristic of cognitive science is that it has moved the study of the mind beyond behaviorism and progressive education and into more productive ways to consider the thinking process involved in problem solving and processing knowledge.

A third characteristic of cognitive science is its utilization of the computer as a fundamental tool in studying how the mind works and brings meaning to learning. The development of computers has also given scientists and researchers the tools to simulate real-world problems through interactive learning systems. These include the interactive video disk and the synergistic merging of various media.[16]

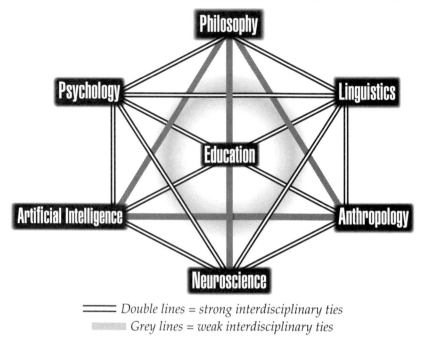

FIGURE 2
INTERDISCIPLINARY CONNECTIONS IN COGNITIVE SCIENCE

Double lines = strong interdisciplinary ties
Grey lines = weak interdisciplinary ties

The key contribution of cognitive science to LogoLearning is its role in lending empirical credibility to ideas that thinkers such as James and Bruner have advocated over the years. In particular, recent studies into brain structure reinforce the LogoLearning contention that connecting content and context application is not only helpful to learning, but essential. In addition, studies in the development of intelligence and the different kinds of intelligence underscore the LogoLearning emphasis that education be focused on the needs of the learner, not the needs of the teacher or the educational institution. Chapter 3 will cover in more detail the connections between brain-based learning research and LogoLearning.

LOGOLEARNING AS REFORM: "FIXING WHAT'S BROKE" IN AMERICAN EDUCATION

Since 1982 American education has undergone the most intense internal scrutiny of its history. If reports and studies alone could improve and change schools and colleges, we would certainly have achieved excellence in education during the decades of the 1980s and 1990s. During this period, summoned by the clarion call from the National Commission on Excellence in Education report entitled, *A Nation at Risk*, at least fifteen major education reform reports and a host of other significant yet less detailed reports appeared. All called for substantive changes in the American education system.

These education reform efforts appear to group around a new set of "three Rs"—reporting, restructuring, and rivalries. Or one could restate these "three R" groupings as "three Cs"—culpability, configuration, and competition.

Reporting: Whose Fault Is It?

In the reporting (culpability) group, the emphasis has been upon achieving accountability through testing, even to the point of developing national tests. An attitude seems to prevail of "Let's find out what students know—or *don't* know—and who we can find culpable for their not knowing. Let's develop a set of [arbitrary] national knowledge standards."

Restructuring: Changing Everything But How We Teach

The restructuring (configuration) group of reform efforts encompasses several diverse proposals, each of which has merit. Restructuring can mean lengthening the school year or the school day. It can involve changing the way student progress is assessed or credit is granted or how students are grouped in classrooms. However, much of the contemporary discussion about restructuring seems to concentrate upon a process called site-based decision making. This initiative is founded on the important belief that those most closely affected by decisions ought to play a major role in making those decisions.

There can be little question that education reform will be more effective when carried out by those responsible for the implementation of that reform. But what's distressing is the small amount of attention that the advocates of this variety of reform seem to give to improving teaching and learning.

Here's an example. The Oregon Educational Act for the Twenty-First Century, established by the 1991 Oregon Legislature, calls for the delegation of school decision making to site committees that are established at the school-building level. A state-level task force worked together to develop guidelines for the operation of these school-based decision-making councils. The guidelines cover such important areas as team building, resource management, changing roles, planning, decision-making processes, respect for diversity, and communication strategies. Not once, however, do these guidelines mention improving the teaching-learning process!

We might expect and certainly hope that site-based groups and their important restructuring efforts will sooner (rather than later) give highest priority to the improvement of teaching and learning. If the restructuring efforts in schools and colleges fail to do this, then we can only wonder if it has been worth the effort.

Rivalries: The Competition Game

In the rivalries (competition) group of reform efforts, the emphasis has been upon words like *choice* or *voucher*. Their efforts are based on the belief that free-market competition between schools will make good schools better and force weak schools to improve. Unfortunately, there is little direct evidence that competition leads to improved teaching and learning.

In 1991 the Carnegie Foundation for the Advancement of Teaching launched an exhaustive study concluding with an exhaustive report entitled *School Choice*. The study involved a year of research; school visits; public polling; and interviews with parents, teachers, and school administrators. From the day the report was issued in October 1992, it attracted enormous media interest, editorial comment, and public attention.

The Carnegie researchers cited several instances where choice initiatives had made a difference; several schools in Minnesota, for instance, had attracted students by creating innovative choice programs. But the study's overall conclusion was that no program had demonstrated a clear link between choice and improving student learning. In fact, the Carnegie report indicates an unimpressive relationship between school choice and learning improvement. For example, standardized test data fail to demonstrate that students who transfer from the public schools to private schools are doing any better in the school of their choice.

I am convinced that school choice at best offers only modest benefits in terms of improving education. If it is not managed carefully—for instance, and the benefits of choice are not available to all—it may even carry harmful risks. But even if it is handled well, I believe the issues of choice must fit into the context of improving learning. It is merely a diversionary tactic to present school choice as a panacea that can miraculously sweep away all difficulties that restrict learning and impede good teaching and enhance student learning.

More of the Same Won't Work!: Taking Reform Behind the Classroom Door

The glaring omission in most of those "how to fix it" reports and discussions has been a lack of emphasis upon teaching and learning—the central mission of education. Although many of the education reform reports have made important contributions to the education enterprise, they have for the most part exhibited a blind spot when it comes to actually changing the way we teach—especially the way we teach students who have previously been classified as "average" in academic ability.

The simple fact is that we can continue to issue position papers on longer school days and years, site-based management, more tests, more reporting, better assessment practices and ignore teaching and learning. None of these reform efforts will make much difference unless we give priority to teaching students more effectively—motivating them to learn and helping them to learn. Reporting, restructuring, and rivalry will not have much influence on what goes on once the instructor closes the classroom door.

Will more of the same lecture/test teaching help prepare a world-class workforce?

Will more of the same classical subject-matter-centered teaching lower the high school dropout rate?

Will more of the same theoretical teaching help students become better connected with real-life problem-solving issues?

Will more of the same teaching help *all* students be winners—not just some of them?

The evidence is strong that the traditional "freezer" approach to education simply isn't cutting it in today's schools. And yet most teacher training institutions are still turning out future teachers who think they must give students "content" 90 percent of the time, with maybe 10 percent of the time spent on application and related meaning. Those teachers who do try to make their instruction concrete and application centered are hampered by school systems and communities who regard hands-on, activity-centered learning as expensive "extras" rather than the backbone of the learning experience. In far too many schools, teachers who want to teach in a more meaningful fashion find they must develop this approach on their own time, with little support from school or community—or, too often, from those bent on reforming our schools.

I am convinced we have too often been working at the margins in our contemporary education reform efforts. Certainly there are salutary aspects to all these reform efforts, but they have not made a significant impact upon overall student learning.

In fact, those students who have been helped most by the education reform efforts carried out over the last three or four decades are those students who *already have* a positive attitude about education. Little has been done for those individuals with negative attitudes—those who see little meaning to their schooling.

A motivation study of how to increase the number of popcorn eaters found that most motivational messages may move an individual who likes popcorn to want more popcorn, but they can do little more. They cannot make a popcorn lover out of someone who is negative about popcorn.[17] Too often, in our reform efforts, we have spent all our time on giving "education lovers" more of the same, but very little effort in changing the minds of those who aren't convinced that education is worthy of their time.

A deep values cleavage lies at the foundation of our educational dilemma. The question is: Do we want to put our resources into educating only the few, or do we want educational institutions to provide meaningful education for all students? The large majority of students who are not likely to earn a four-year baccalaureate degree see little meaning or value in their current education experiences. Yet education reform efforts too often advocate just more of the same . . . and *more of the same* is not the answer.

Renate and Geoffrey Caine make this pungent observation in their insightful book, *Making Connections:*

> If students are to become genuinely more proficient, more capable of dealing with complexity and change, more highly motivated, and more capable of working both autonomously and with others, then we have no choice but to teach for meaningfulness."[18]

If education reform is to move beyond the margins, we must make fundamental, systematic changes in how we approach the teaching-learning process. Whether we title our efforts "LogoLearning" or "situated cognition"[19] or "anchored instruction" or "experiential learning" or "cognitive apprenticeship" makes little difference as long as many, many educators continue to explore, research, discuss, and practice bringing meaning to the education experience for more students.

---

[1] Viktor Frankl, *Man's Search for Meaning: An Introduction to Logotherapy,* trans. Ilse Lasch (Boston: Beacon, 1963), 164.

[2] Frankl, *Search for Meaning,* 120.

[3] Arthur Applebee, Judith Langen, and Ina V. S. Mullis, *Crossroads in American Education* (Princeton: Educational Testing Service, 1989), 26–40.

[4] Applebee, Langen, and Mullis, *Crossroads,* 40.

[5] Theodore B. Sizer, *Horace's Compromise: The Dilemma of the American High School Today* (Boston: Houghton Mifflin, 1984).

[6] Douglas Dickston, "The Pen Pal Letter: A Separate Audience," *Innovation Abstracts,* 15 (no. 23, 1993).

[7] Edwin M. Bridges, *Problem Based Learning for Administrators* (Eugene: University of Oregon, ERIC Clearinghouse on Educational Management, 1992), 14–15.

[8] John Bransford et al., "New Approaches to Instruction: Because Wisdom Can't Be Told," *Similarity and Analytical Reasonings* (Cambridge: Cambridge University Press, 1989), 470-497.

[9] William James, *Talks to Teachers on Psychology* (New York: Norton, 1958), 41.

[10] James, *Talks to Teachers,* 68.

[11] For an excellent analysis of behaviorism as well as an introduction to cognitive science, see Sylvia Farnham-Diggory, *Cognitive Processes on Education* (New York: Harper-Collins, 1992).

[12] John Dewey, "Morals and Conduct," *The World's Great Thinkers: The Social Philosophers* (New York: Random House, 1941), 461.

[13] John Dewey, *The Ingles Lecture* (Cambridge: Harvard University Press, 1931), 1.

[14] Jerome S. Bruner, I. J. Goodnow, and G. A. Austin, *A Study of Thinking* (New York: Science Editions, 1956).

[15] Bruner, *Toward a Theory of Instruction* (Cambridge: Harvard University Press, 1966).

[16] Dale Parnell, *Dateline 2000: The New Higher Education Agenda* (Washington: Community College Press, 1990), 241.

[17] Mary Anne Raywid, *The Ax-Grinders* (New York: Macmillan, 1963).

[18] Renate and Geoffrey Caine, *Making Connections: Teaching and the Human Brain* (Alexandria: Association for Supervision and Curriculum Development, 1991), 172.

[19] For an interesting article on situated cognition see J. S. Brown, A. Collins, and P. Duquid, "Situated Cognition and the Culture of Learning," *Educational Researcher* 18 (no. 1, 1989), 32–41.

CHAPTER 2

What Are We Trying to Accomplish Here?

Maintaining Constancy of Purpose

Education is affected by larger trends — forces beyond the classroom and the campus that determine, inevitably, the destiny of our schools. No debate about the nation's schools can be conducted without reference to the larger context within which each school carries on its work.

–Ernest L. Boyer, President Carnegie Foundation for the Advancement of Teaching

*H*ave you ever watched a slide show that was slightly out of focus? Didn't you want to adjust the projector focus knob to clarify the picture?

That's the way I feel sometimes when I review the goals of some educational organizations. All too often they are vague, fuzzy, unrealistic, or simply irrelevant. More important, they fail to focus on the vital question: Just what are we trying to accomplish here? As a result, there is little congruence between purposes and outcomes.

Developing purposeful goals for educational organizations and then keeping those goals clearly in focus is a key challenge for leaders at all levels of education. These mission-statement goals must serve as the basis for building common understanding and commitment in all levels of the organization. They must be vital and dynamic statements against which *all* education practices within the organization may be judged. But when that is not the case—when the goals of that organization are fuzzy or inadequate—the actions of the institution tend to exemplify the same fuzziness.

I have found relatively few instructors and administrators in educational institutions who are focused and articulate about the goals and purposes of their school or college. That doesn't mean they don't have goals. In almost every educational institution, in fact, you can find a carefully prepared document setting forth the goals of the organization. There may even be an organizational mission statement. But these documents are seldom well connected, in any direct way, to the actual work of the institution: teaching and learning. Instead, goals discussions sometimes appear to serve as a kind of intellectual sauna bath for educators. People feel warm and good discussing all of those profound platitudes, but the stated goals fail to make much of a difference in how teachers teach, how students learn, and how the whole process relates to the community at large.

In 1984, Vito Perrone, Dean of the Center for Teaching and Learning at the University of North Dakota, led a team of scholar-educators in a high-school visitation project for the Carnegie Foundation for the Advancement of Teaching. Fifteen high schools representing a diversity of location, size, community, social class, and racial distribution were elected for intensive observation. One of the most pertinent observations to come out of these visitations had to do with goals. In general, Perrone and his team observed,

> the schools struggle for a consensus about purposes. Seldom, for example, do teachers and administrators, students, and parents come together to discuss seriously their purposes in relation to the particular groups of young people served by a school. Few of the teachers and administrators we met were particularly articulate about purposes. . . .

Not surprisingly, they also observed that

> Structurally, curriculum appears very much as it has been for most of the last fifty years. . . . There is a sameness about how teachers approach their teaching. The format is fairly conventional, text-book oriented, information filled. . . . We saw very little inquiry teaching, and problem-solving skills did not tend to be taught.[1]

The observations of Perrone and his associates match my own views, distilled from forty-plus years of experience at nearly all levels of education. Most schools and colleges, with the exception of those with strong specialty concerns, seem to lack a unified sense of purpose, a clear sense of exactly what they are supposed to be doing.

THE PROBLEM WITH EDUCATIONAL GOALS

The problem with many educational goals statements is that they are often so vague or general that they have little meaning and give weak direction for curriculum development. Such statements as "improving the condition of humankind" or "producing well-educated citizens" may be good for political speeches but provide little concrete guidance to the teach-ing-learning process.

Another common problem with many educational goals is that they are out of date; they fail to reflect current societal realities or the real needs of the majority of students. Far too many of our current educational goals, practices, and requirements are based upon the needs of a society of ninety or one hundred years ago. In many ways, young people and their needs have outgrown our present-day schools and their goals statements.

One state board of education, for example, states that it is the singular goal of high-school vocational education to prepare students for entry-level jobs, and that only students placed directly into jobs after high school (not those going on to some kind of postsecondary education) can fulfill that stated purpose! That goal is totally out of touch with the realities of a workplace that requires increasingly higher levels of training. Isn't it ironic that a state policy would quash the efforts of students who become so "turned on" by learning that they wanted to continue to study in a particular field to increase their competencies and reach higher career goals?

THE QUESTION OF PURPOSE

The deeper problem here, of course, is that many educational goals and mission statements seem to be singularly unconnected to the real world in which most students will spend the majority of their lives. One reason people are so dissatisfied with modern education is that we have failed to match in any systematic way the goals of education with the competencies required to function successfully in our modern society.[2]

That brings us to the real, underlying issue, that of *purpose*. Too many mission statements limit their goals to listings of desired ends or outcomes and fail to address the underlying questions of "Why are we here?" "What are we trying to accomplish?" "How does our mission relate to the contemporary needs of our students?"

At the historic 1989 education summit in Charlottesville, Virginia, the President of the United States and the governors of the various states declared that "the time has come, for the first time in U.S. history, to establish clear national performance goals, goals that will make us internationally competitive. We must become a nation that values education and learning." This group called for the restructuring of the education system around national education goals.

AMERICA'S EDUCATION GOALS
By the year 2000 . . .

1. All children in America will start school ready to learn.
2. The high school graduation rate will increase to at least 90 percent.
3. American students will leave grades four, eight, and twelve having demonstrated competence in challenging subject mat-

ter including English, mathematics, science, history, and geography; and every school in America will ensure that all students learn to use their minds well, so they may be prepared for responsible citizenship, further learning, and productive employment in our modern economy.

4. Students will be first in the world in science and mathematics achievement.
5. Every adult American will be literate and will possess the knowledge and skills necessary to compete in a global economy and exercise the rights and responsibilities of citizenship.
6. Every school in America will be free of drugs and violence and will offer a disciplined environment conducive to learning.[3]

This was an important effort; it helped move the subject of education to a much higher national priority than ever before in United States history. The only problem with these national goals is that they focus exclusively on anticipated or desired outcomes without actually addressing the underlying purpose of education.

This is a rampant problem with educational mission statements and goals, whether at the national, state, or local level; there is little consensus about what educational institutions are supposed to be doing. As a consequence, the teaching-learning process is not linked in any direct way to overriding purposes and goals. We still teach math for math's sake and science for science's sake and the like. We still expect students to sit still in a class, listen to a lecture, memorize their notes, and spit the information back on a test.

American students will not become first in the world in science and mathematics achievement just because the President of the United States and the governors have stated this as a desired outcome of the educational effort. Something else must happen! We must first develop a clear and strong sense of purpose, then build our desired outcomes around these purposes.

The total quality management ideas of W. Edwards Deming[4] have exerted a powerful and transforming influence in the business community, and I applaud the growing interest among educators in these ideas. Unfortunately, however, efforts to implement TQM concepts in education have tended toward the external and marginal, aimed more at administrative and personnel operations than at the actual teaching-learning process. TQM concepts have yet to make a significant impact on the classrooms or the curricula of American schools and colleges. I believe it is time they did.

The top Deming recommendations for any organization are, first, to maintain a vigorous constancy of purpose, and second, to be sure everyone and every effort of the organization is aimed at those purposes. To Deming, excellence is not a product, but a process, a way of doing things. The Deming and TQM concept of excellence addresses the connection between purposes and outcomes, between theory and practice, between knowing and doing, between content and the context of application.

The key for Deming is the link between purpose and action—and that is a primary point of establishing goals. The modern curriculum and contemporary practices of teaching cannot remain unconnected from the overall purposes of education in the vain hope that somehow it will all connect for the student.

School and college organizations, to be effective, must have a sense of purpose that is widely shared by students, teachers, administrators, board members, parents, employees, and the community. Educators, parents, and students alike must capture a clear vision of what we are supposed to be accomplishing in our educational institutions. Unless the institutional actions reflect and support the institutional purposes, those purposes have little chance of effectively shaping the future of the organization.

WHAT IS THE PRIMARY PURPOSE OF EDUCATION?

This, of course, raises another basic question, one which I have already touched upon: What *is* the appropriate purpose of an educational institution? Should schools, especially public schools, be primarily in the business of instilling facts and developing so-called intellectual skills, or should they have a more practical focus as well, preparing students for the "real world" of careers, grocery stores, marriages, and the like?

American education has always tended to favor the concept of a "classical subject-matter education" in the tradition of the Greek philosopher Plato over the more practical, problem-oriented approach favored by Aristotle. In fact, an important body of leaders in this country today holds that the term *education* refers only to the development of the intellectual proficiencies and the dissemination of knowledge. Others—myself among them—hold to a broader definition of education that includes an understanding of how knowledge may be applied to real-life situations. This dichotomy in educational philosophy may be at least a partial source of the continuing dilemma over the appropriate purposes of education.

The late Keith Goldhammer, former Dean of the College of Education, Michigan State University, and long-time observer of the American educational scene effectively sums up the split and points toward a healing sense of purpose that transcends it:

> The establishment of a public-school system in the United States based upon the Platonic intellectual tradition has tended toward an elitist conception of its functions, has emphasized its selective characteristics, and has at least partially abrogated its

responsibilities for the seventy-five to eighty percent of its students who by native ability, interest, and aspiration are identifiable with the practical affairs of our culture rather than inclined toward the more abstract and conceptual activities of the academic disciplines. . . . That which is needed in today's world is neither a new brand of academicism nor a new style of vocationalism, but a fusion of the two."[5]

African American history provides a dramatic example of the ongoing tension between Plato and Aristotle in education—and its contemporary legacy. The great educators Booker T. Washington and W. E. B. DuBois spent much of their lives debating the issue of the academic goals versus practical goals, education for the few and education for the many.

DuBois was interested primarily in educating academically talented black young people, believing that these students, if well educated, would then teach and lead the masses. Washington emphasized education for the masses, self-employment, and the need for black young people to work with both their heads and their hands. He believed that "the Intellectuals," as he called them, understood theories but were not knowledgeable enough in practical matters to become well-educated artisans, business people, and property owners.

In later years DuBois came over to Washington's position. But it was too late to turn the tide; DuBois' earlier position had gained the ascendancy. This is one reason that in Washington, D.C., a city that is 70 percent African American, the concept of vocational education has generally received the cold shoulder. The District Board of Education allotted less than 4 percent of its 1990 budget to the vocational high schools, which enroll more than 10 percent of the high school students.

And there is the lingering feeling in the African American community that any form of practically oriented education represents something inferior.[6] When Washington Technical Institute was merged with the University of the District of Columbia, it didn't take long for many of the two-year technical-education programs to be phased out as "unfitting for a university curriculum."

But this attitude isn't limited to the African American community; it pervades our country. Isn't it amazing that we honor modern dance as something worthy of college credit but look down on self-defense for a law enforcement officer as unworthy? We deem welding-as-art as worthy of university credit, but consider occupational graphic arts as unworthy of college credit.

There is nothing inherently wrong with a classical education for those relatively few students who learn well utilizing abstract and theoretical approaches to learning. However, to say that *all* students must experience a classical education is akin to saying all students should wear a size ten shoe. And the reality of our challenging age is that *all* students must experience a deeper and more meaningful education than we have ever known in our history.

We have what might be called the 20-80 problem in education. The 1990 United States census revealed that only 20 percent of adult Americans (twenty-five years and older) hold a four-year baccalaureate degree or higher. Even though the specific numbers may vary from community to community, such a statistic makes us face up to the fact that the large majority of Americans do *not* now and are unlikely in the near future to hold a four-year college degree. In much of our educational practices, however, we indicate in all kinds of subtle (and not so subtle) ways that the only road to educational excellence is the road leading to a four-year college degree—usually the classical Platonic education. What a waste of human resources! The baccalaureate degree is a perfectly appropriate goal for some individuals, but *all* students should feel they are on the road to excellence rather than just some of them.

What then is the appropriate purpose that should drive the goals of educational institutions? If we believe it should be the primary purpose of education to help each student become a fully competent, contributing, self-motivating, self-fulfilling member of our society, then it is time to redirect our goals discussions toward a broader, more inclusive view.

INFORMATION RICH, APPLICATION POOR

James S. Coleman has called the society of one hundred years ago "information poor but experience rich."[7] People received most of their information from parents or neighbors or at best a few newspapers and books. But they were involved in all kinds of hands-on work experiences. From an early age, most children were given responsibilities or chores from which they learned practical skills and gained experience.

Today we live in a different society, an information-rich but relatively experience-poor society. Adults and children alike are bombarded with data from books, newspapers, magazines, radio, and especially television. In fact, many children receive much too much data too soon, before they are emotionally equipped to assimilate or interpret all they see and hear without the personal experience that provides realistic perspective. They may witness brutal scenes of wartime combat before they have seen a dead rabbit or suffered the loss of a pet dog. When they enter the classroom they are confronted with even more information, often as randomly presented as and generally less interesting than what they have received on television.

This fundamental societal shift, I believe, calls for a corresponding shift in our educational goals and makes a more practical, purposeful orientation even more critical than ever before. Whereas schools of a hundred years ago might have been justified in their purpose of imparting knowledge to children already rich in experience, today's schools must take on the task of helping students bolster their information with experience.

How, then, can educational institutions provide an education as rich in experience as in knowledge, an education that will enable students to relate their education to the experiences and responsibilities that constitute a part of living for all of us? That question points to a key aspect of LogoLearning goals: to provide an education that connects information and knowledge with real-life experiences. Young people of today and tomorrow need an application-rich as well as an information-rich educational program.

By giving young people an experience-rich education, we may solve several problems indirectly. Traditionally, we have tried to attack emotional, racial, ethical/moral, and cultural problems by telling people what to do—telling them to be moral, for example. But education must be more than telling. It must provide opportunities for students to experience and cope with real situations—to be able to apply knowledge and to feel a sense of responsibility for their own actions.

Through helping students understand the connection between human commonalties and their education, for instance, students of tomorrow can begin to feel more confident about themselves. In the process, they can develop tolerance toward others through developing the skills required for coping with a real life filled with human diversity. Thus, an experience-rich education can provide students with esteem-building experiences to enable them to act as independent, contributing citizens. I believe the purpose of providing an experience-rich education must play a crucial role in shaping the goals of today's educational institutions.

SCHOOLING FOR LIFE

The competencies required to cope with real-life roles and their relationship to the curriculum are crucial issues facing education today. These issues are interrelated, and the measure by which they are made compatible will largely determine the significance of all education activity. The fact that educational institutions are busy and teachers are skilled does not necessarily mean that these institutions are accomplishing the right things.

Three fundamental questions must be asked of all educational institutions: What are your education purposes? Which real-life needs are you meeting? Is there a sense of congruence among and between purposes, actions, and outcomes? These questions must be posed continually when we attempt to assess institutional effectiveness. They must be crucial to shaping the institution's goals.

It is common for students to know more about the ice age and the Incas than they do about their own city council, the property taxation system, the justice system, or even voting in elections. Most young people haven't the foggiest idea who levies the taxes that support their own schools or colleges and how or why they are levied.

As we examine the changes in our society over the past seventy-five years, we find that in our highly urbanized society some citizenship problems are apparent that were not apparent when an individual could ride a horse to the county seat. For example, we don't talk much in our schools about citizenship on our streets and highways, yet more than forty thousand people are killed annually in traffic accidents, and any mention of driver training is viewed as a "frill."

During my tenure as Superintendent of Public Instruction in Oregon, an excellent curriculum guide on local and state governments was published by the State Department of Education. I was visiting a high school one day, and I asked an American history and civics teacher, "How do you like the curriculum guide on local governments?" The reply was, "Oh, I'm not using it. I'm too busy teaching about the federal government. I just don't have time to get into state or local government."

Our curricula and textbooks are filled with emphasis on the federal government. Our students must know about the United States Constitution and the Bill of Rights, but we just don't seem to have time to do much with local and state governments, the governments closest to the people.

I am *not* saying that teaching students about the federal government is unimportant. I am just trying to illustrate the tremendous lack of congruence between what we emphasize in education and the competencies required to cope with modern life, even in the area of citizenship. To put it bluntly, real life often feels mighty uncomfortable in the school and college environment.

What is the alternative? LogoLearning aims at bridging the gap between school and life and providing an experience-rich education by building educational goals around *life roles* and *human commonalities.*

LIFE ROLES, HUMAN COMMONALITIES, AND LOGOLEARNING GOALS

What are those human activities that most people have in common—the involvements that bind us together as a people? While we are all different, at the same time we have similar basic needs and perform certain basic functions in society.

Each of us, for example, no matter what our specific interests, talents, or backgrounds, must find some way to provide ourselves with the necessities of life. Each of us, for instance, must earn wages or produce income in some way. Each must purchase or otherwise procure the necessities of life, must live in relationship to other people, must confront and adapt to change.

Each of us, in other words, must function in a variety of roles throughout our lifetime, and the requirements of these various life roles present a promising beginning point for setting educational goals. LogoLearning calls these basic functions "human commonality roles" and uses them to formulate educational goals with a clear view of the basic purpose of education. (Similar approaches are called "skills for living" or "life-role education.")

A human commonality role can be described as a life role that most individuals perform throughout their lives. The specific aspects of each role are shaped by the expectations that an individual and others have for it as well as by certain norms that society in general attaches to it. And successful performance in life roles requires more than knowing a certain set of facts or even acquiring a certain set of academic skills. It even requires more than *telling* students about the roles. Instead of helping students acquire chunks of knowledge in arbitrary subject areas, LogoLearning aims at helping them acquire the skills and information they need to live as successful human beings in the real world.

This does not mean that students shouldn't receive information relating to the roles they must fill in life. But it is vital to recognize that they are *already* living those roles every day and in fact are experiencing life roles with or without the kind of education that will enable them to achieve a measure of success and fulfillment—yes, even survival—in those roles.

What are the human commonalities that form the basis for LogoLearning goals? Obviously, these can be categorized several different ways, but I would isolate seven great human commonality strands that run through the education curriculum. These are the life roles of:

1. Lifelong learner,
2. citizen,
3. consumer,
4. producer,
5. individual (self)
6. family member,
7. aesthetic/leisure participant.

The first four strands probably represent the primary areas of accountability for educational institutions; schools take responsibility for helping students gain the skills and knowledge they need to be lifelong learners, citizens, consumers, and producers. Educational institutions share accountability with the home, the church, the media, and governmental agencies to help individuals develop the competencies to function effectively as family members, become self-renewing individuals, and develop an appreciation for what is good, beautiful, and true. Figure 1 suggests a LogoLearning purposes paradigm around which an educational curriculum can be structured.

FIGURE 1
LOGOLEARNING GOALS PARADIGM AND LIFE ROLE COMPETENCIES

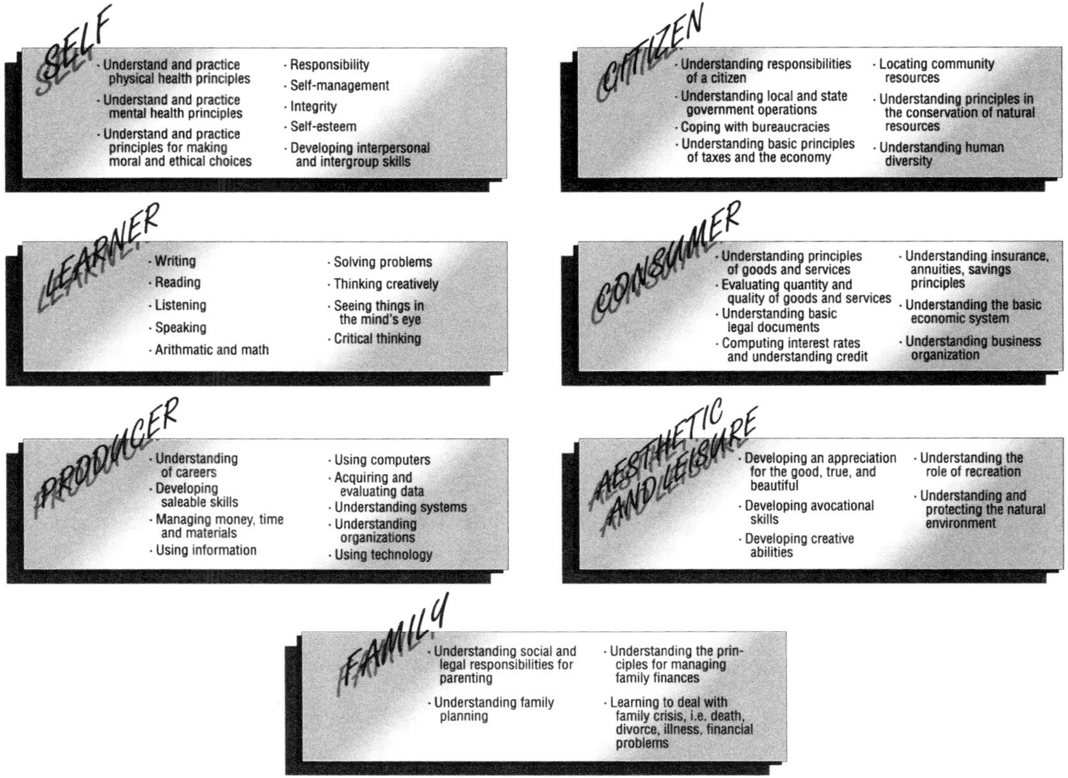

SELF
- Understand and practice physical health principles
- Understand and practice mental health principles
- Understand and practice principles for making moral and ethical choices
- Responsibility
- Self-management
- Integrity
- Self-esteem
- Developing interpersonal and intergroup skills

CITIZEN
- Understanding responsibilities of a citizen
- Understanding local and state government operations
- Coping with bureaucracies
- Understanding basic principles of taxes and the economy
- Locating community resources
- Understanding principles in the conservation of natural resources
- Understanding human diversity

LEARNER
- Writing
- Reading
- Listening
- Speaking
- Arithmetic and math
- Solving problems
- Thinking creatively
- Seeing things in the mind's eye
- Critical thinking

CONSUMER
- Understanding principles of goods and services
- Evaluating quantity and quality of goods and services
- Understanding basic legal documents
- Computing interest rates and understanding credit
- Understanding insurance, annuities, savings principles
- Understanding the basic economic system
- Understanding business organization

PRODUCER
- Understanding of careers
- Developing saleable skills
- Managing money time and materials
- Using information
- Using computers
- Acquiring and evaluating data
- Understanding systems
- Understanding organizations
- Using technology

AESTHETIC AND LEISURE
- Developing an appreciation for the good, true, and beautiful
- Developing avocational skills
- Developing creative abilities
- Understanding the role of recreation
- Understanding and protecting the natural environment

FAMILY
- Understanding social and legal responsibilities for parenting
- Understanding family planning
- Understanding the principles for managing family finances
- Learning to deal with family crisis, i.e. death, divorce, illness, financial problems

43

SOME CHARACTERISTICS OF LOGOLEARNING GOALS

In addition to being based on human commonalities, here are some essential characteristics of LogoLearning goals:

Characteristic #1: LogoLearning Goals Are Application Oriented.

In LogoLearning, student competence is defined as demonstrated ability to understand and *apply* knowledge. Therefore, embedded deeply within the philosophy of LogoLearning is the idea that every student must have the opportunity not only to acquire knowledge, but also to develop the competencies required to function effectively in his or her real-life roles. Thus, there is a profound shift in emphasis from *what is to be taught* to *what is to be learned.* This is probably the most basic and powerful characteristic of LogoLearning goals: They are application oriented.

One great problem for modern education is a lack of congruence between the traditional time-honored subject-matter disciplines and the competencies required to function successfully in our human commonality life roles. Our daily lives simply do not fall into the neat categories of math, social science, English, and science, although skills and knowledge traditionally tied to these disparate areas certainly apply to the requirements of daily living.

LogoLearning goals, in essence, serve as a learner-centered bridge between these disciplines and the competencies an individual needs to succeed in contemporary society. They embody information-rich and application-rich purposes for education that are based upon human commonalities.

Characteristic #2: LogoLearning Goals Are Learner Centered.

American educational institutions operate within a web of tensions. The major strand in this web of tensions is the relationship between individual (and society) needs and the goals and activities of the schools. Much of what is done by the American educational institutions is done well, but the key question is: Should it be done at all? Are our educational institutions addressing the highest-priority *needs* of the student at large, or are they addressing the needs of the administration and faculty or the subject-matter discipline?

What part of the school and college curriculum, for example, is responsible for helping people learn about dealing with their local government, voting on tax proposals, working with planning commissions? Where is the specific accountability in the modern school curriculum for helping a person develop the competencies to become a lifelong learner—to analyze, to improve his or her problem-solving abilities? Too often, educational institutions leave such vital concerns to chance and continue to insist on meeting the student at the point of some arbitrary subject-matter need rather than at the point of real-life human commonality needs.

Characteristic #3: LogoLearning Goals Make a Clear Policy Demand.

The second major characteristic of LogoLearning goals is that they make a clear policy demand; that is, they require action on the part of the institution. Educators seem strangely reluctant to talk about policy demands, but the education enterprise is chaotic unless policy demands are made upon the educational system, with purposes clearly stated. Every quality organization or system requires clear statements of purpose or mission. When these are vague, out of focus, or simply missing, the institution will respond inconsistently and probably inadequately to needs and challenges that arise. Some clear purpose policy statements are required.

A goal-based policy demand provides the framework for establishing, conceptualizing, and integrating the processes and procedures of LogoLearning. Here is an example of the kind of clear statement policymakers might consider writing into a policy handbook for public schools:

> The education of the student results from a combined effort of home, church, community, schools, and the media. It shall be the responsibility of our schools to help students develop individual competencies to function in the life roles of lifelong learner, individual, producer, citizen, consumer, family member, and aesthetic leisure-time participant.

The schools have an important but shared responsibility and a secondary role in helping students develop social, emotional, cultural, and ethical/moral values. It is important that the schools support and reinforce the home and other community institutions in these areas.

The first priority for the use of schooling resources shall be to help students develop the competencies to function as lifelong learners.

This type of mission statement not only begins to make a policy demand upon the system, but also begins to define areas for which schools can be held accountable. Educational leaders must make decisions that are congruent with this policy directive. Educational institutions must deal with goals and purposes that they are uniquely equipped, by training and by financing, to accomplish. But under the current system, educational institutions are often held accountable for outcomes and results they haven't the remotest possibility of achieving. A clear policy statement helps to clarify what is expected of the institution.

Characteristic #4: LogoLearning Goals Are Time-Flexible.

LogoLearning is not as interested in how long it takes a student to master a given competency as in mastery itself. As a result, LogoLearning goals provide for considerable flexibility when it comes to scheduling. Less emphasis is placed upon completing a specified unit of study in a specified time period. Students are allowed to move and recycle through the instructional process easily, and time is used flexibly. Not all learners are nine-week or eighteen-week learners; in fact, rate of learning is one key difference among learners.

The specific implications of a flexible time policy are many. Why shouldn't high schools develop basic skills labs that are open long hours of the day and on weekends? Math, reading, and writing labs operated on an open entry-open exit basis are standard fare in most community colleges. These labs are usually supervised by paraprofessionals, teaching assistants, or even volunteers working under the supervision of professional teachers.

Why can't the school days be shortened and the school year lengthened? Extending the school year from the usual thirty-six weeks to forty weeks but shortening students' school day by one hour might give teachers more daily time to do their work and to collaborate with other teachers and students. (European schools have long ago gone to the longer-year and shorter-day routine.) It would also allow teachers more opportunity for professional development. In the current time-packed environment and with the present organizational pattern, there is little time left for teacher collaboration on pedagogical issues.

Another important benefit that a flexible time schedule could play is increased opportunity for staff development. Most major corporations provide far more time for staff development activities than educational organizations do. Setting aside time for inservice days, workshops, and consultation with colleagues not only would promote more effective teaching, but would also boost morale and provide sorely needed encouragement. As faculty and staff from different institutions met together, closer ties would develop between schools, colleges, and universities—especially between teacher-training facilities and schools. Yet this kind of activity also requires time, particularly much-needed consultation time with master teachers. In the current environment and organizational patterns, there is little room for teachers to reflect on pedagogy or collaborate as students of teaching. Making room for this kind of activity will require rethinking how we structure the school day and school year in terms of time.

Characteristic #5: LogoLearning Goals Are Purpose Centered and "Up Front."
A fifth characteristic of LogoLearning goals is that clear statements of purpose must precede expected outcome statements and must be placed "up front" as guides for both instructors and learners. There should be no surprises in the instructional or evaluation process. The instructional program is designed around certain goals, and the measurement and evaluation process occurs when learners demonstrate the ability to meet clearly defined outcome requirements related to these purposes.

For example, when teaching swimming, the instructor teaches to the test by having the student swim from one end of the pool to the other. The goal and purpose are learning to swim. Being able to swim across the pool is one clearly anticipated outcome. The students know ahead of time the purpose of the lesson and the expected outcome. There are no trick questions or surprises.

The same can be said for computing interest rates, reading a newspaper, locating information in a library, or interpreting the Bill of Rights. LogoLearning does not turn its back on traditional subject matter or on time-honored instructional techniques; it only insists that the instructional program be based upon clear purposes and that students be required to demonstrate how what they have learned applies to those purposes.

This aspect of LogoLearning goals helps to correct a common problem encountered with stimulus and response behavioral objectives—their narrow focus. Behavioral objectives tend to keep teachers and learners so focused on the minuscule that the connection is never made to the larger purposes of a lesson or the even larger purposes of the educational organization. LogoLearning insists that no matter what is being taught, students should always know how that subject matter fits into larger purposes.

Transforming Schools through LogoLearning Goals

How might schools be different if LogoLearning beliefs and strategies were accepted?

First of all, principals, faculty members, administrators, and other educational leaders would view their primary task as providing constancy and continuity of purpose for the school team and continuously seeking better ways to fulfill this purpose. It is the job of the leader to connect the parts with the whole. The primary task of a LogoLearning educational leader is not controlling, but connecting purpose with action.

The LogoLearning leader understands that quality teaching and learning depend on the ability of the school staff continually to identify and meet the learning needs of students as related to the commonly agreed-upon purposes of the school. The LogoLearning leader realizes that the never-ending process of improving teaching and learning requires the active involvement of all staff members. The whole school staff must constantly be studying and proposing how to improve. But as followers of the TQM ideas have shown in other organizations, improvement must always be connected to a common understanding among all members of the team that purpose, action, and outcomes can never be separated.

Transforming Elementary, Middle, and Secondary Schools
Through a Human Commonalities Orientation

As an illustration of how LogoLearning goals can change the face of

American education for the better, let us examine how schools might prepare students for one of the life roles we listed earlier—that of wage earner or producer.

First, I want to reemphasize that LogoLearning is not synonymous with occupational or career education, although I am convinced that the latter is a significant motivational aspect of education. American education has suffered from a misunderstanding of the place and value of career education. Unfortunately, the image in the minds of too many people is that career education involves only specific job training—teaching students to repair automobiles or cut hair. But career education in the LogoLearning mold encompasses much more; it is simply a way to help individuals develop the competencies they need to be wage earners and producers. It is one of, but only *one* of, the human commonality goals of LogoLearning.

When the LogoLearning goal of preparing students to be wage earners or producers is connected to teaching, then lessons of all different kinds—math, science, reading, writing—are infused with practical examples from the world of work.

Even students in the primary grades can be helped to see some relationship between what they are learning and the ways they might someday use those skills in the their jobs or careers. Indeed, where practiced, contextual teaching in the elementary schools brings more life, more meaning, and more rigor to these early school experiences. Some elementary schools, for example, have developed readers and library collections around world-of-work and career themes.

In the middle grades, connecting the LogoLearning life role of producer with the teaching and learning process can also bring new purpose to those difficult early adolescent years. In most middle schools, career exploration is part of the schooling experience, but this often involves little more than having students visit businesses in the community or talk about jobs with a counselor or teacher. The most effective career exploration, however, involves a rigorous multidisciplinary approach (perhaps with industrial arts and homemaking teachers leading the way) that integrates career exploration with math, science, English, and social studies.

Studying the building of a house, for example, can be an application-rich experience. Teachers not only talk about the occupations involved in mixing mortar and cement; they also help students actually lay up a few bricks and experience the mixing of mortar (and talk about the chemistry of mortar). But that isn't all. The illustration of constructing a building provides tremendous opportunities for social studies. Who planned the house and how was the planning done? Who gave the permit to build the house? How was the money raised to pay for the building? What math is involved in building something?

There are hundreds of contextual learning examples that could be utilized to bring life experiences to the curriculum. Ideally, at the end of a three- or four-year period in the middle school, students will have explored all the major career clusters or families of occupations and have had hands-on lab experiences related to various aspects of these occupations.

Transforming Higher Education

LogoLearning goals are not just for elementary, middle, and secondary schools; they can also inject a new sense of purpose into college curricula. Community, technical, and junior colleges will find a LogoLearning orientation especially beneficial when developing institutional mission statements.

The Dallas County Community College District (DCCCD) in Dallas, Texas has developed a Skills for Living program that shapes the basic curricular purposes of that large system of community colleges. After extensive review by faculty and administrative committees, nine common learning goals have been developed and adopted. These clearly reflect a human commonalities orientation:

1. *Living as a Learner:* Each DCCCD college will provide students opportunities to develop learning skills (reading, writing, speech communication, and computation) through assessment, advisement, and instruction.
2. *Living with Yourself:* Each DCCCD college will provide direction and opportunities for students to become more competent in developing themselves as individuals.
3. *Living with Others:* Each DCCCD college will provide direction and opportunities for students to become more proficient in establishing and maintaining satisfying relationships with others.
4. *Living with Environments:* Each DCCCD college will provide opportunities for students to understand the relationship between individuals and their environments and make responsible decisions about the use of natural, human, technological, and spatial resources.
5. *Living as a Producer:* Each DCCCD college will provide opportunities for students to become more competent producers.
6. *Living as a Consumer:* Each DCCCD college will provide opportunities for students to become more competent as consumers.
7. *Living in the Community:* Each DCCCD college will provide opportunities for students to become more competent in using their skills and initiative to serve their local, national, and world communities and improve their quality of life.
8. *Living Creatively:* Each DCCCD college will provide opportuni-

ties for students to become proficient in the assessment, development, and application of their creative abilities.

9. *Living in the Future:* Each DCCCD college will provide opportunities for students to become more proficient in anticipating and accommodating change and to become more competent in examining possible alternatives for the future.

The Dallas County Community College District faculty has recognized that many common learning goals were already addressed throughout the curriculum, but it was difficult for faculty or students to determine with any degree of precision just how the goals were being met. (This is a common experience for schools attempting to restructure their curricula around the LogoLearning philosophy.) It was felt that the "Skills for Living" goals could best be attained by building learning requirements around the human commonalities theme. This has required the maintenance of several delicate balances throughout the college program:

- The development of basic literacy skills, conceptual skills, and lifelong learning skills is fundamental to common learning in the community college, aimed at helping students live with greater proficiency and humanity.
- One important goal of a community-college education is to help students develop the competencies required for work in high-performance workplaces.
- The connection must be made between the structure of the curriculum, which reflects the common goals, and the process of integrating this learning through continuous curriculum review and evolution of the teaching-learning process.
- The breadth and specificity of course and program content must relate to the human commonality goals and anticipated outcomes. Educational institutions must acknowledge student differences by offering learning and content choice balanced with a common core of learning for all students.[8]

Assessing Competencies: The American Walkabout

Approaching educational goals from a human commonalities, life-roles perspective raises a variety of interesting possibilities for schools at different levels. For instance, schools might want to take a new look at how achievement is measured. Perhaps new high school graduation requirements or certificate of initial mastery standards should be designed so that the student would demonstrate he or she has developed the competencies required to function in a modern world.

Such a process could be likened to the Australian aborigine's custom of a "walkabout," a survival test that marks the transition from childhood to adulthood. Perhaps schools should be asking: What corresponding competencies would an American young person need to survive and succeed in the adult world? Can the rite of passage be something more than the driver's licence exam?

While the Australian aborigine youth stands watch as part of tribal duty, perhaps the American youth should be required to demonstrate that he or she can read a ballot and rationally explain the impact of a yes or no vote on civic measures. While the young Australian aborigine learns to survive by stalking wild game, perhaps the American youth should demonstrate that he or she has acquired sufficient survival skills to function as a wage earner in an increasingly complex and technical world. In the wilderness of the Australian outback, the young aborigine must recognize signs of direction or be lost. The American youth must demonstrate the survival skills to function as a wise consumer in a wilderness of credit cards and easy credit or be financially lost.[9]

THE POWER OF PURPOSE-DRIVEN GOALS

Whatever specific policies they influence, LogoLearning goals are the beginning point in making meaning the focal point of education at all levels. As educational leaders begin to bring a greater degree of congruence between purposeful goals, anticipated outcomes, and the teaching-learning process, the work of creating a continuous and coherent learning experience for students becomes easier. At the same time, students are empowered to develop their competencies to higher levels and become more capable of coping with complexity and change. But for all this to happen, leaders, teachers, and policy-makers alike must keep a clear and constant vision of what education is supposed to accomplish in the long run, and constancy of purpose must be the driving force behind all educational goals.

---

[1] Vito Perrone, *Portraits of High Schools* (Lawrencevillle: Carnegie Foundation for the Advancement of Teaching, Princeton University Press, 1985), 645–650.

[2] For more information on the human commonalities theme, see Ernest Boyer, *A Quest for Common Learning* (Princeton: Carnegie Foundation for the Advancement of Teaching, 1981).

[3] United States Department of Education, *America 2000: An Education Strategy Sourcebook* (Washington: Government Printing Office, 1992), 1.

[4] A. Gabor, *The Man Who Discovered Quality* (New York: Penguin, 1990).

[5] Keith Goldhammer and Robert Taylor, *Career Education: Perspective and Promise* (New York: Charles E. Merrill, 1972), 21.

[6] Pat Press, "It's Not Dirty Work," *Washington Post*, 27 May 1984.

[7] James S. Coleman, "The Children Have Outgrown the Schools," *Psychology Today*, February 1972, 72–84.

[8] For more information on the Skills for Living program, contact the chancellor of the Dallas County Community College District, 701 Elm Street, Dallas, Tex. 75202.

[9] For more information on the walkabout idea see Maurice Gibbons, "Walkabout: Searching for the Right Passage from Childhood and School," *Phi Delta Kappan*, May 1974, 596–602 and Dale Parnell, "The Oregon Walkabout," *Phi Delta Kappan*, November 1974, 205–206.

CHAPTER 3

The Touchstones of Reality

Teaching Students the Way They Learn

The student who can begin early in life to see things as connected has begun the life of learning. The connectedness of things is what the educator contemplates to the limit of his [or her] capacity
–Mark Van Doren

*Q*uestion: What is the greatest sin committed in today's schools?

Answer: The failure to help the student make *connections*—

- between information and experience,
- between school and the world,
- between one subject-matter discipline and another;
- between his/her past knowledge and present challenges, his/her present challenge and future responsibilities.

And why is such a failure so critical? Because *connections* are what students desperately require to survive and succeed in our high-speed, high-challenge, rapidly changing society.

A NEW EDUCATION FOR A NEW WORLD

The past one hundred years have seen an almost incredible array of changes. In my own brief lifetime I have gone from cow chips (farm work) to potato chips (home chores) to computer chips (word processing) to nanochips (high technology and miniaturization). At the same time, my country and my world have experienced enormous upheaval and absorbed turbulent changes.

Think about it. In the course of a century we have had one major war that introduced the use of the airplane and bombs falling from the sky. We have had another major war where we introduced the atomic bomb that can blow up entire cities. We can now travel faster than the speed of sound, even into space, and experience instant visual communication around the world. We have indeed become a global community in terms of trade, travel, and telecommunications. The computer is revolutionizing the publishing industry, the defense industry, the financial world, health sciences, basic manufacturing, and the information industries. Securing up-to-date information on complex matters is now almost an instantaneous process.

The past hundred years have transformed the face of technology—and that technology has transformed us. What would life be like for young people of today if the inventions of the past one hundred years were to disappear— no automobiles, no airplanes, no telephones, televisions, computers, CD players, VCRs, air conditioning, shopping malls, or electronic games? Neil Postman makes this insightful observation: "When you plug something into the wall, someone is getting plugged into you. Which means you need new patterns of defense, perception, understanding, and evaluation. You need a new kind of education."[1]

And what kind of education prepares children for their information-rich, experience-poor, high-octane world? Once again, they need instruction and curricula that help them understand, process, and use the information hurled at them from all directions. They need hands-on, concrete experience that gives them confidence in their ability to cope. They need both guidance and practice in solving problems and setting priorities. In short, they need an education that serves as a touchstone of reality, helping them make connections in an often disconnected world.

We are in good company when considering that people learn best from experience; such great thinkers and innovators as Alfred North Whitehead, Maria Montessori, Howard Gardner, William James, and of course Jean Piaget have said exactly that. Piaget in his studies of childhood development made much of the fact that children are always endeavoring to make that connection and attempting to understand how things work and what people do.[2]

But that's not what happens in many contemporary classrooms. Instead, they are confronted with even *more* information and knowledge in forms that are often as random and disconnected—and considerably less interesting— than what they get outside of school.

How then can teachers provide experiences that will enable students to connect knowledge with the real-life experiences that constitute a part of living for all but a few of the most challenged? That is the key question that LogoLearning endeavors to answer. In fact, the chief characteristic of the LogoLearning approach is that all good teaching is unmistakably contextual, aimed at helping students make connections. It therefore gives the student a touchstone of reality upon which to build solid, meaningful learning.

MAKING CONNECTIONS IN A DISCONNECTED WORLD

Making sure that education is a touchstone of reality is especially important in view of the distorted versions of reality our culture tends to promulgate. Television is a prime culprit in this regard, with hours of programming that present wealth as the key to happiness and violence the key to success.

Such programming offers young people a world of questionable values and instant gratification, with heroes who are always attractive, do little work to pay for their pleasures, and do not seem responsible for their own actions. Media often manufacture celebrities and package these individuals as heroes. While examples of selflessness and courage abound—policemen, firefighters, social workers, generous entrepreneurs, teachers, and others—they are little noticed or celebrated.

Daniel Boorstin comments pointedly upon this modern phenomenon: "We have used our wealth, our literacy, our technology, and our progress to create the thickets of unreality which stand between us and the real facts of life. . . . transforming us from travelers into tourists."[3]

Can it be that we do not have just an education problem, but a reality problem in our country? Adults and children alike seem disconnected from some of the most important and basic realities of how our society functions. Ernest Boyer, President of the Carnegie Foundation for the Advancement of Teaching, relates this story:

> When I was United States Commissioner of Education, Joan Cooney, the brilliant creator of *Sesame Street*, came to see me one day. She said they wanted to start a new program at Children's Television Workshop on science and technology for junior high school kids, so they could understand a little more about their world and what they must understand to live. It subsequently was funded and called "3-2-1 Contact." In doing background work for that project, they surveyed some junior high school kids in New York City and asked such questions as: "Where does water come from? A disturbing number said, "the faucet." And they asked, "Where does light come from?" They said "the switch." And they asked, "Where does the garbage go?" "Down the chute." Their sense of connectedness went about as far as the VCR, the refrigerator door, and the light switch in the hall."[4]

We Live in an Interconnected World

At the same time that such distortions of reality pervade our culture, our nation and our educational institutions are caught up in a closely woven web of real-life connections. These connections and relationships are already at work, knitting something that looks like a fishnet. A cell here and a cell there are tied together by strands of information or cooperation or just individual contacts.

This interconnectedness can make problem solving seem confusing or even impossible. Take for example the issue of improving the United States economy. A high-performance economy depends upon the development of a high-performance workforce . . . but the needs of our workforce have been neglected by our educational institutions. Superior manufacturing relies on top-flight research and development, but there are signs that our nation is losing our once-commanding lead in technological innovation and technology transfer. Economic and civic success in this learning age depends upon well-educated citizens at all levels of the population spectrum, but the educational shortcomings of our school systems have been amply documented.

Time after time, when discussing one issue, we find ourselves pulled to zero in on others. A discussion of developing a world-class economy almost inevitably turns toward the problems of inadequate education or our lack of global awareness. Discussions of inadequate education, in turn, inevitably raises economic questions.

The positive side of this connectedness issue, of course, is that improvements in one sector of society can positively affect other sectors as well. Growth and improvements in whole industries such as financial services, computers, communications, biotech research, and manufacturing will have a multiplier impact across many other industries, improving their profitability and productivity. The impact of developing high-performance workplaces will then spread out across the country in thousands of new and different ways.

Most of our national leaders now agree that the key issues of society must be addressed simultaneously. We simply cannot afford to solve problems one at a time in an unconnected way. Our system must interact synergistically, with each part of the system considering its impact on other parts.

Today's interconnected economy emphasizes the importance of an interdisciplinary education and the development of broad skills. High-performance workers of the future must be able to handle projects from start to finish, from the definition of system requirements through project management.

Manufacturers are now predicting a rapid shift from assembly-line production to smaller units with smaller suppliers involving fewer workers with the abilities to do more complex things. This will require "hands on" managers, project leaders, and frontline workers able to roll up their sleeves and work as a team. It will also demand workers who have higher skills and greater flexibility than ever before—and who have the ability to retrain quickly for new jobs.

The occupational half-life, or the time it takes for one-half of workers' skills to become obsolete, has declined over the past decades from seven to fourteen years to three to five years. Workers at all levels of the workforce require literacy skills and cognitive skills that enable them to function as lifelong learners and adjust to new work situations. In an interconnected society, an education that helps students make connections is not a luxury.

MASLOW AND LOGOLEARNING CONNECTIONS

Abraham Maslow's theory of basic human needs has been highly influential in educational circles because of the insight Maslow provided into human motivation, which includes motivation for learning. Maslow contended that human beings are motivated by several basic needs. These needs are intrinsic and generic and are organized into a hierarchical order on the basis of urgency and priority. Throughout his or her life, said Maslow, a person is always desiring something and is satisfied completely for only brief periods. As each desire is satisfied it is replaced by another. Most individuals in American society have partially satisfied many basic needs, but other unsatisfied needs continue to motivate and drive them. Maslow found that individuals who satisfy their basic needs are healthier, happier, and more effective, while those whose needs are frustrated often develop psychopathological symptoms.[5]

According to Maslow, the most powerful and basic need is for *survival*, both physiological and emotional. Maslow indicates that once the survival needs are satisfied to a degree, safety needs emerge. Any good teacher of young children knows that the child needs a secure world. When security and a degree of consistency are absent, the child becomes anxious. With a preponderance of survival and safety needs met, the needs for love and belonging emerge. Another level of need revolves around at least two kinds of esteem needs—self-esteem and respect from others. Self-esteem needs include feelings of competence, confidence, achievement, and independence. Finally, after adequate satisfaction of the esteem needs, the need for self-actualization generally emerges. This highest level of need stems from that constant human drive to explore and expand the human potential.

MASLOW'S HIERARCHY OF HUMAN NEEDS

What does a hierarchy of needs have to do with making connections and learning for meaning? Simply put, the need for meaning and connections applies at *all* levels of the needs hierarchy, not only at the top. Human beings are always endeavoring to bring to or find some meaning in their circumstances. As Viktor Frankl discovered in the concentration camp, even people whose physical survival is in question, who must battle for the basics of food and shelter, are still motivated by the need to make connections and find meaning in their lives!

This urge is what Viktor Frankl calls the "will to meaning" and what Abraham Maslow regards as "man's primary concern." Indeed, Frankl and Maslow[6] agreed that the will to meaning is the *overarching survival need* for all human beings. The distinction between the two is simply a matter of means and ends. The will to meaning is the end, the "what for," the "why." Meeting the hierarchy of needs is the means to the end—and the two must connect.

Food, for example, is essential for survival, yet food alone does not bring meaning to life. A safe neighborhood is needed to bring a sense of safety, yet a feeling of safety does not bring meaning to life. Feeling that we belong and that someone cares about us is fundamental to good mental health, but belonging alone does not bring meaning. Indeed, meaning becomes a survival issue.

Human needs are indeed motivational in nature and must be met, at least partially, in rank order, but this urge to get needs met must be aimed at connecting with the survival need of meaning. American education institutions often aim at the self-actualization and higher-level needs while ignoring the real-life competencies required for an individual to function successfully as a lifelong learner, citizen, consumer, wage earner, or family member. Linking the fulfillment of real-life needs with learning for meaning is part of the LogoLearning connection.

SEARCHING FOR CONNECTEDNESS IN DISCONNECTED SCHOOLS

In a society that is simultaneously disconnected and tightly interconnected, schools can make the difference. They can help students develop the discernment they need to challenge distortions of reality and develop the broad perspective necessary to handle a web of interconnected problems and possibilities. Schools and colleges can and should help students make connections of their own, using their minds to connect content (acquisition of knowledge) with context (application), with understanding (assimilation), and with problem solving (association).

Unfortunately, for the most part, that simply is not happening in many classrooms.

Many of the most pressing issues in our society, for example, have no home in the typical education curricula and time-honored subject-matter disciplines. Where is the curricular responsibility for discussing the improvement of intergroup race relations? Where is the curricular home for studying the physical environment? (In biology? In chemistry? In physical science? In political science?) What discipline has the responsibility to study the drug-abuse problem or the AIDS epidemic? (Health classes? Biology classes? Social studies classes?)

Granted, these issues might be covered in any number of classes. And granted, some students will manage to make the connections on their own; there have always been students who seem to learn with almost no input from the educational system. Still, there seems to be little deliberate effort to connect the disciplines and organization of the education curriculum with the tough multidisciplinary issues of real life.

What do we have instead? Typically, we have allowed the theoretical subject-matter emphasis of the typical college prep/baccalaureate degree curriculum to be the sole definition of excellence in education, despite the fact that 75-80 percent of the students in a typical school system will not likely complete a baccalaureate-degree program. (This group of students has been called "the neglected majority."[7])

How does teaching and learning proceed in the typical secondary and postsecondary classroom? The content of education is compartmentalized into subject-matter disciplines. Students in schools, even students in colleges and graduate schools, are asked to learn innumerable facts and unrelated information sufficiently to do well on important tests.

In the first chapter of this book, we described this as the "freezer method" of education; the unspoken direction is "Put this knowledge into your mental freezer and freeze it on the basis that you might use it someday." Learning isolated dates and places in history, memorizing isolated formulas in mathematics and science, learning the names of parts of organs and organisms in isolation are all examples of this approach to education.

Paulo Freire uses a different metaphor; he compares the typical classroom of today with banking. The teacher deposits information into the student and the student memorizes the knowledge well enough to pass a test but with little understanding of how that deposit of knowledge might be used. "Banking education anesthetizes; it attempts to maintain the submersion of consciousness."[8]

Students have ways to avoid memorizing "freezer" or "banked" knowledge because they see little value or use in what they are asked to store in their mental vaults. If students do not see some application for the knowledge being presented they will not usually work hard enough to learn that material beyond short-term memorization. Some will cheat. And while we cannot condone cheating, it will likely continue as long as a majority of students, even academically talented ones, believe that much of the current academic curricula is not worth the effort it takes to learn it.

A recent edition of *The Oregonian,* a statewide daily newspaper in Oregon, reported on a national survey recently released by Who's Who Among American High School Students. The survey showed that:

> nearly 80 percent of the nation's top high school juniors and seniors those with a B average or higher not only believe cheating is widespread but also have cheated themselves in one way or another. Of the 1975 students surveyed, 67 percent said they copied someone else's homework, 40 percent said they cheated on a test or quiz, 25 percent said they used summaries to avoid reading books, and 14 percent said they had plagiarized parts of

an essay. . . . Students say some teachers invite cheating through weak classroom management or poor instruction. Matt Dickey, 17, a student council member at Benson High School in Portland, said some classes were so boring that kids resorted to cheating just to get by so they could devote more time to interesting classes.[9]

It would be difficult to convince me that high school students are any less ethical than their adult role models. But after talking with many high school students, I have gotten one message loud and clear. Most high school students see little meaning in much of their courses of study, and consequently they reason (wrongly) that cheating does not seem so bad. They reason that they will soon forget most of what they are tested on, so what difference does it make if they cheat or not?

A letter to Ann Landers from a student and published nationwide in her syndicated column illustrates, with tongue in cheek, how the freezer approach works in the eyes of the student.

Test Prayer
Now I lay me down to study,
I pray the Lord I won't go nutty.
If I should fail to learn this junk,
I pray the Lord I will not flunk.
But if I do, don't pity me at all,
Just lay my bones down in the study hall.
Tell my teacher I did my best,
Then pile my books upon my chest.
Now I lay me down to rest
And pray I'll pass tomorrow's test.
If I should die before I wake,
That's one less test I'll have to take.
Sufferin' Student[10]

Disconnected Systems

The connectedness issue runs through our school systems as well as through our communities and our world. For example, college and university leaders seem to be discovering that their students had a life before college and that their institution's roots grow deep into the soil of the secondary and elementary schools. Yet there has been precious little communication between college and high school faculty and few efforts at smoothing the transition from secondary to postsecondary schools. For easier articulation to take place for students—and *articulation* is a form of *connection*—the inner walls of separation within the academic community must be broken down.

This applies equally to walls of separation between various "kinds" of education. The distrust will never melt away until genuine conversation between and among various groups of teachers begins. Yet even today we still talk about *vocational* education and *academic* education as though they exist in separate worlds, and vocational educators and academic educators act that out on a daily basis.

No longer can the debate of the importance of the liberal arts or career programs be allowed to degenerate into an either/or argument. They are *both* important, and the technological-learning age demands balance between the two. Educational excellence at all levels must be defined in terms of connectedness, continuity, and applicability that combines knowing with doing.

THE BRAIN CONNECTION

The need for connectedness in education goes even deeper than the pressures of contemporary society or the demands of the workplace. The very process of learning itself calls for connections—unless connections are made, little effective learning takes place.

Psychologists, philosophers, and educators from William James to Jerome Bruner have made the case for connections in education. In the past few decades, brain research has shown that the need for such connections is rooted in the basic function of the brain itself. When we teach for connectedness we are teaching in accordance with the way the human brain operates.

Experience and the Brain

We now know that experiences and environment shape our brains and therefore condition our ability to learn. Our experiences help condition our brains, and our brains help condition our experiences. We cannot afford to disconnect brain development from real-world experiences or separate brain development from life experiences.

The human brain is a wondrous biological instrument consisting of many interconnected parts. Functionally speaking, these can be divided into three major systems.

The smallest and most primitive system of the brain consists of the brain stem or lower brain, which controls automatic body functions such as breathing and heartbeat, and the cerebellum controls muscular activity and balance. Most biologically driven behavior can be traced to these two structures, which we can think of collectively as the "automatic reflex brain."

The second part of the brain is the limbic system, or "memory" brain, which is concerned especially with memory, emotions, and motivation. It includes the hippocamus, which plays a large role in memory-related learning; the thalamus, which relays information from the senses to the cerebral cortex; the hypothalamus, which controls sexual urges and other motivation;

and the amygdala, which controls anxiety and fear. The third part of the brain is the cerebrum, or "thinking brain," which fills the entire upper part of the skull. It is composed of a soft, wrinkled outer layer called the cerebral cortex and an underlying mass of connected nerve fibers. This part of the brain controls and connects the higher functions of learning, judgment, and intelligence.

THE AMAZING, INTERCONNECTED BRAIN

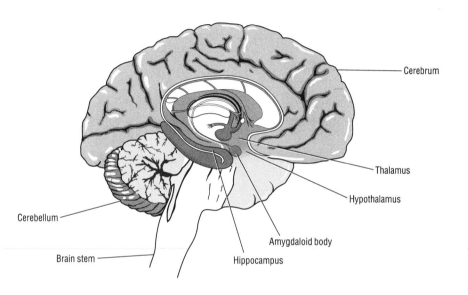

Experiences Affect Brain Development

One of the most compelling reports on brain research comes from researchers at the University of California, Berkeley. In examining the brains of animals over a long period of time, these researchers discovered a direct relationship between life experiences and brain development. The brains of animals who lived in an enriched environment were found to actually weigh more than those of animals from a poor environment. The Berkeley researchers concluded from this and other studies that the environment can make a significant difference in the development of the animal brain and that the brain maintains the ability to grow and develop over a lifetime.

The jury is still out as to how, or how much, experience affects the development of the human brain. An increasing body of research, however, indicates a connection between experience and brain development:

> We now have evidence to illustrate the details of the anatomical changes that do occur with modification in the environment. This

evidence addresses many of the questions that concerned the early sociologists and educators, including the effects of the environment on the young as well as the elderly, sex differences, and the effects of nutritional deprivation, isolation, or crowding. It is now clear that the brain is far from immutable.[11]

We know that students change both physically and psychologically as they grow and experience life. We also know that students from enriched home environments seem to have an increased ability to learn. Since the brain is a physiological organ, it seems reasonable to hypothesize that the physical structure of the brain can change as the result of experience and that an educational environment as rich in experience as in information can have a positive impact upon brain development.

The Brain Is Interconnected

An amazing aspect of the human brain is its ability to receive impulses and simultaneously to send many messages. An individual brain cell may be connected to ten thousand or more other brain cells. Without going into the intricate workings of dendrites, axons, and synapses, we can get a sense of this simultaneous message operation by saying that an individual nerve cell receives messages from other nerve cells and "decides" to pass the message (or nervous impulse) along, depending basically upon the amount of the electrical charge behind the message. When it finds no connection, the message is not sent.

It is important to note here that nerve cells exist throughout the brain, and all three parts of the brain, as well as both right and left hemispheres, interact in mysterious ways. Even though we do not understand fully how the brain interacts, it is clear that behavior, emotions, perceptions, ideas, recollections, and thoughts influence and condition each other. It is this interconnectedness, particularly the connection between memory, emotion, perception, and rational thought that intrigues the educator. For the most effective learning and the higher levels of thinking to take place, the "three brains" must operate together.

What about the left brain/right brain propositions which posit that individuals tend to be right-brain or left-brain dominant? According to these theories, the right-brain dominant person tends to see the whole before the parts and is good at intuitive processing. The left-brain dominant person tends to reduce information into parts and be a sequential and linear learner who prefers analytical thinking. Some teaching methodologies have been based on these hemispheric differences in the brain.

But what has often been overlooked in the right brain-left brain discussions is that the two hemispheres of the brain are linked together and both are involved in all activities involving the whole person. The left and right brain are connected and they interact continuously. Accordingly, the teaching-learning process must involve the parts and the whole in connected, meaningful, and relevant learning experiences.

The Brain Discards Meaningless Information

Another pertinent fact we do know is that the brain tends to discard information for which it finds no connection or meaning or for which the meaning is obscure. The brain is designed to perceive patterns and connections, and it resists having meaningless patterns of knowledge imposed upon it.

Every time an individual achieves something (regardless of age) or experiences something that "connects" with a previous experience or a perceived value, that achievement or experience will tend to "stick"—and something will be learned. The reverse of this is true for experiences that don't connect or hold any perceived meaning.[12] (Is it any wonder that one fourth of our public school students do not complete their high school education? They drop out in part because their brains will not allow them to repeat meaningless learning over and over again.)

UCLA's Madeline Hunter, the well-known author of *Elements of Successful Instruction* and many other publications, often demonstrates this characteristic of the brain by giving participants in her teacher workshops four successive lists to learn:

- a list of nonsense syllables like "mef" and "lif,"
- a list of unrelated words like "dog," "fan," and "see,"
- a list of related nouns like "coat," "sweater," and "pants,"
- a list of related words in grammatical order, such as "A girl went...."

Workshop participants quickly realize that each succeeding list is easier to recall than the previous list. Hunter then points out that there is little inherent meaning in material alone, but meaning comes from an interaction between the individual and the material, and the context of use. Her advice to teachers is that the more the material can be made meaningful to the student, the more easily it will be assimilated into the cognitive structure and the better they will recall it.[13]

This leads us to an observation of profound significance for teaching. For teaching to be truly effective, the student must be motivated to connect the content of knowledge with the context of application, thus developing the ability to solve problems and to assimilate that knowledge in a way that can be useful in new situations.

Please do not misunderstand. This is not to say that all experiences must be "fun" for meaningful learning to take place. Learning is not just a bottle of happiness pills. But learning at all times should be meaningful. It should utilize the brain's large capacity to make the connections between content and context, with the result of a satisfying learning experience.

The Brain Can "Downshift"

Based upon the various contemporary theories of how the brain functions, I have come to believe that the brain responds differently to different stimuli and that various teaching methods may cause a student to shift learning from the thinking brain to the memory brain or even to the automatic-reflex brain. What this means is that a great bit of contemporary education begins and ends with the memory and automatic-reflex brains, with the thinking brain left to rest.

A system of teaching based upon rewards, punishment, narrowly preconceived outcomes, and time limits may cause students to "downshift" in the use of their brains. Under the threat of a failed test or a low grade, or in a timed learning situation, the student will tend to call upon the memory brain for help rather than the thinking brain. But in order for the student to see meaning and to make as many connections as possible—for long-term learning to take place and higher-order thinking skills to develop—the thinking brain must be involved. This means the learner must be engaged or involved in an examining, questioning, viewing, valuing, and interactive process. Lesson plans and lectures in which all learning outcomes are determined in advance deny the brain the opportunity to discover the information, organize it, connect it with individual past experiences, and therefore create tailor-made meaning for that individual.

BARRIERS TO CONNECTEDNESS IN SCHOOLS

The point is clear: An effective education is one that focuses on real-life connections. And so the question is obvious: What stands in the way of a more "connected" education for students in American schools? Several substantial barriers stand in the way.

First, the contemporary demands on educational institutions, and upon teachers, are mammoth and often unrealistic. Time constraints, administrative directives, and community pressures often force teachers, particularly elementary/secondary school teachers, to choose between what they know is good teaching and survival as a teacher. Current efforts aimed at requiring national tests and national teacher certification may bring even greater pressure upon teachers to emphasize the "freezer" approach and further entrench an outmoded pedagogy.

Second, the educational enterprise has remained essentially unchanged over the past hundred years. We have standardized tests and textbooks that do little to connect content with context, a standardized system of semesters and hours that does not recognize individual differences in learning speeds and styles, standardized teacher certification unrelated to how a teacher performs in a classroom—all enacted with good intentions, but generally ignoring learning for meaning with real-world situations in mind. These standardized methods and approaches have in many ways become the jail from which pedagogy has been unable to escape.

Probably the greatest barrier to teaching for meaning is the pressure to "cover the material" mindset. In my experience, most teachers prefer to teach for meaning. But many teachers fear (with reason) that connecting subject-matter content to real-world experiences will not allow time to cover all the material in the textbooks or follow the curriculum guide. The need to get through a certain prescribed amount of material presses teachers and students alike to fall back on stuffing material into the "freezer" rather than developing active thinking and connected learning.

Some teachers also fear that introducing the elements of discovery and experience into the classroom will cause them to lose control of students. It is certainly vital to maintain an orderly learning environment. But teachers and educational leaders at all levels of education are beginning to see that teaching within context and making connections need not mean chaos. In fact, a "connected" education which helps students learn within the context of application results in a more interested and responsive classroom. After all, who will be more disruptive—a student who is absorbed in an experiment or one who is bored with a lecture?

> ## BARRIERS TO CONNECTEDNESS IN SCHOOLS
>
> **1.**
> CONTEMPORARY DEMAND ON EDUCATION INSTITUTIONS AND TEACHERS
>
> **2.**
> EDUCATIONAL ENTERPRISE HAS REMAINED ESSENTIALLY UNCHANGED
>
> **3.**
> PRESSURE TO COVER MATERIALS
>
> **4.**
> FEAR THAT INTRODUCING ELEMENTS OF DISCOVERY INTO THE CLASSROOM WILL CAUSE THEM TO LOSE CONTROL OF STUDENTS
>
> **5.**
> BEHAVIORIST APPROACH TO TEACHING

Yet another barrier to connectedness in our schools is the essentially behaviorist approach to teaching that has become entrenched in many of our classrooms. Many classroom techniques, for example, rely upon the behaviorist approach of practice, rehearsal, reward, and punishment, with a beginning, middle, and end to a behavioral objectives lesson. We have raised a few generations of individuals upon a reward and punishment basis, training them to work only for a grade or some immediate reward. ("Will it be on the test?" is familiar classroom litany.)

Most of the current testing and assessment practices are aimed at surface knowledge, with little attention given to how that knowledge is required. This emphasis upon surface knowledge fails to capitalize upon the awesome capacity of the thinking brain to make connections. A student may memorize the formulas for determining surface area and determining angles, use those formulas correctly on a test, and thereby achieve the behavioral objectives set out by the teacher. When confronted with the need to build a shed or wallpaper a room, the same student may well be left at sea because he or she hasn't made the connection between the formulas and their real-life application.

I am not saying that the behavioral approach has no place in teaching or advocating that educators throw out all behavioral objectives and lesson plans. Stimulus-response approaches and even "freezer" memorization can be helpful or even necessary to instill certain kinds of learning, especially those requiring more or less automatic responses. At the same time, the behaviorist approach should not be the only teaching method used, and it should not be used for those areas of study that require higher level thinking processes.[14]

TEACHERS MAKE THE DIFFERENCE

Clearly something has to change in our schools, and I believe that change must focus on the issue of connectedness. Educational policymakers and leaders can issue reams of position papers on longer school days and years, site-based management, more achievement tests and better assessment practices, and other "hot" topics of the moment, and it will not make much difference in what students know and can do. The difference will be made when classroom teachers begin to connect learning with real-life experiences in new, applied ways and when the reformers begin to focus upon connecting teaching with learning for meaning.

Cognitive science research has proven over the past twenty-five years that a large majority of students learn best if taught using the applied learning method in which they are encouraged to explore and experiment and in which content is related to a clear purpose. As stated by Sue Berryman and Thomas Bailey in their work entitled *The Double Helix of Education and the Economy*:

> Traditional education and training misses the point that human beings are inquisitive, sense-making animals who learn best when they are fully and actively engaged in solving problems that mean something to them. Because it violates the way that people learn most effectively, our current approach to education and training simply does not work.[15]

If the numerous reports on how to "fix" American education are any indication, most educational leaders have yet to grasp the complexity and effectiveness of teaching and learning for meaning. This pretty much leaves it up to the classroom teacher to deal with the issue. And yet the educational system in our country could be vastly improved if all of us who are involved in the art and science of teaching could understand the breathtaking power of the brain to make meaningful connections and the limited power of the brain to deal with material that does not connect.

What a difference it can make if teachers stress connected knowing over segregated knowing, understanding over memorization, the problem-solving model over the freezer or banking model, and thematic teaching over the "cover the textbooks" approach. Teaching conducted upon the connected model will help students develop the "aha" spirit as well as the alert mind. It will help them learn with their whole brain, involving all their mental processes. And it will help students develop the mental tools they need to survive and succeed in our complex, interconnected society.

TEACHING FOR THE COMPUTER AGE

The complexities of our changing society demand that teachers become far more than dispensers of knowledge. And this is true not only because teaching for meaning and connectedness is more effective, but because computer technology will eventually consign "banker" or "freezer" teaching methods into the archives. Computer and related artificial intelligence devices are fast developing into a pervasive information and knowledge system. The information age is upon us, and computer-based information designs are helping students move more swiftly up the skill ladder, helping students learn more things more effectively. If a teacher is considered little more than a knowledge dispenser, that teacher can easily be replaced.

Computer devices are rapidly becoming faster, smaller, and more powerful. In 1990 it was estimated that five million components could be placed on one silicon chip. (In 1985 it was one million.) By the year 2000 it is expected that one chip will hold some *one billion* components. As soon as chips can be stacked one above the other, a solid cube of transistors can potentially be developed to rival the human brain, at least in circuit and connector capacity.

Computer devices not only are exponentially growing in number and sophistication, but are emerging as key providers of information, even as the growth of formal knowledge is increasing. The emerging Integrated Services Digital Network (ISDN) is a vast network of data and information going around the world as an interconnected system.[16] The high volume of knowledge and information being generated is generally beyond the capacity of the human brain to keep up.

As a consequence of all of this development, the teacher of today and especially of tomorrow must be more, much more than a knowledge giver. More than ever, the teacher's role must be that of *connector*. Instead of serving as an information bank, the teacher must serve as a kind of symphony conductor who directs students through the complex interactions of knowing and doing. The computer can supply the information, but it remains up to the teacher to help students discover the *meaning*.

Teachers must have a depth of knowledge. But even more important, the teacher must know how to apply that knowledge to bring about understanding and aid problem solving. He or she must provide the LogoLearning link of connectedness that students desperately need in this information-rich, even information-glutted computer age. ♀

---

[1] Neil Postman and C. Weingartner, *Teaching As a Subversive Activity* (New York: Dell, 1969), 7.

[2] P. A. Cowan, *Piaget with Feeling: Cognitive, Social, and Emotional Dimensions* (New York: Holt, Rinehart and Winston, 1978), 11.

[3] Daniel Boorstin, *The Image: A Guide to Pseudo Events In America* (New York: Macmillan, 1988), 54.

[4] Ernest Boyer, unpublished paper from the Carnegie Foundation for the Advancement of Teaching, November 1991.

[5] Abraham Maslow, *Motivation and Personality* (New York: Harper & Row, 1954).

[6] For more information on this subject read Viktor Frankl, *The Unheard Cry for Meaning* (New York: Simon and Schuster, 1978). In this book, Frankl specifically discusses Maslow and even relates comments made by Maslow about Frankl's theories. Both Maslow and Frankl believed their two approaches connected without contradiction.

[7] Dale Parnell, *The Neglected Majority* (Washington: Community College Press, 1985).

[8] Paulo Freire, *Pedagogy of the Oppressed* (New York: Seaview, 1971), 68.

[9] Bill Graves, "Student Cheating," *The Oregonian*, 21 October 1993.

[10] Printed 16 August 1993 in the *Salem* [Oregon] *Statesman Journal*.

[11] M. Diamond., *Enriching Heredity: The Impact of the Environment on the Anatomy of the Brain* (New York: Free Press, 1988), 2 and Bennet et al., "Chemical and Anatomical Plasticity," 610–619.

[12] For more information on the brain see R. Ornstein and F. F. Thompson, *The Amazing Brain* (Boston: Houghton Mifflin, 1984) and P. D. MacLean, *A Mind of Three Minds: Educating the Triune Brain*, the 77th Yearbook of the National Study of Education (Chicago: University of Chicago Press, 1978). Paul MacLean, the former director of the Laboratory of the Brain and Behavior in the U.S. Institute of Mental Health, has developed what he calls the "triune brain theory" suggesting three parts to the human brain. These involve the reptilian brain, which relates to the overall automatic maintenance of the body and to physical survival; the limbic brain, which houses the major center of emotions and feeling; and the neocortex, which houses most of the brain physiology and controls writing, speech, and thinking processes. This theory parallels our analysis of the three brain parts and their mysterious actions.

[13] Ronald J. Gentile, *Instructional Improvement: Summary and Analysis of Madeline Hunter's Essential Elements of Instruction and Supervision* (Oxford: National Staff Development Council, 46).

[14] For in-depth information on the brain and learning, see Renate Nummela and Geoffrey Caine, *Making Connections: Teaching and the Human Brain* (Alexandria: Association for Supervision and Curriculum Development, 1991). The ASCD has also developed a Brain-Based Education Network to foster dialogue about these issues. For information call 1-703-549-9110, #502 or #506. Or write the Association for Supervision and Curriculum Development, 1250 Pitt Street, Alexandria, Va 22314.

[15] Thomas Bailey and Sue Berryman, *The Double Helix of Education and the Economy* (New York: Institute in Education and the Economy, Columbia University, 1992.

[16] For more information on this subject see P. N. Johnson-Laird, *The Computer and the Mind: An Introduction to Cognitive Science* (Cambridge: Harvard University Press, 1988).

CHAPTER 4

The Best for Everyone

Toward a New Understanding of Excellence

You see, really and truly, apart from the things anyone can pick up (the dressing and the proper way of speaking, and so on), the difference between a lady and a flower girl is not how she behaves, but how she's treated. I shall always be a flower girl to Professor Higgins, because he always treats me as a flower girl, and always will; but I know I can be a lady to you, because you always treat me as a lady, and always will.

– George Bernard Shaw,
Pygmalion

*H*ow many times have you heard some educational leader talk about the "pursuit of excellence" in education? To *pursue* something means to follow or to chase it for the purpose of overtaking or capturing it. If you accept this definition, here is a key question for you: How many educators across the country are actually breathless from chasing an elusive educational excellence, as though excellence were an object to be captured?

I believe the metaphor is inappropriately used and has led education down a dead-end road. Excellence cannot be caught as a wild animal is caught. It can only be cultivated, challenged, and celebrated, like a flower growing in enriched soil and nurturing sunlight. To cultivate something means to prepare for its growth and to improve its growth through attention and labor.

Have you ever heard of a school or college using the slogan "Cultivating Excellence"? Probably not! But it does bring to mind a subtle but crucial question for those of us dedicated to education as a profession. Are we "chasing" or "cultivating" educational excellence?

How we answer this question makes a difference, because much of our educational philosophy and teaching-learning strategy will flow from the answer to this question. To pursue leads to external actions: capturing to tame, building fences to control, labeling to identify, and feeding to maintain. To cultivate leads to internal actions like growth, improvement, and maturing.

We are often confused about the key issues in searching for educational excellence. Whether a high school sends all or most students to college;

whether a community college specializes in college transfer courses over technical education; whether a university stresses the liberal arts over career courses; whether the students are black, brown, or white; young or old; men or women—these are not the key issues in cultivating true educational excellence.

What does matter is making sure that our efforts at excellence involve seeking the best for *all* students, not simply labeling and sorting the so-called smart students from the pack and shining the spotlight on those few.

LABELED BY THE BELL

The great symbol of American education has been and continues to be the bell-shaped curve, which is based primarily on the assumption that 20 to 30 percent of our population is born with the innate ability to learn higher-level cognitive skills. At the earliest levels of formal education, instruments like the IQ tests, which primarily measure verbal and mathematical abilities, are used to identify where a student may fit on the bell-shaped curve. On this basis we label students as bright or gifted or college bound, average or general, and slow or learning deficient.

This view of student intelligence and ability has led education into labeling students using words like "able and gifted" (smart), "ordinary" (average), "special needs" (slow), and "reluctant learners" (troublemakers). Such labels lead us to false images of students. A labeled (stereotyped) image can obliterate or at least fog up our reality and experience.

FIGURE 1
THE BELL-SHAPED CURVE

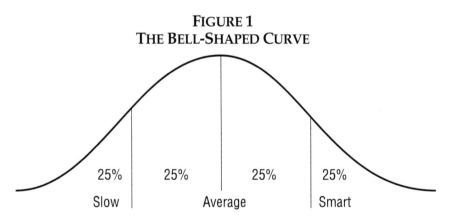

Excellence in education is not a matter of identifying and sorting the "good" from the "not-so-good" students. For too long we have followed a factory-model education that has been designed to sort out the so-called smart students from the slow students and then concentrate our limited resources upon the few winners who will complete a college-baccalaureate-degree program and become the leaders in our country.

Excellence in education has been traditionally measured by IQ tests, grade levels on academic achievement tests, college entrance exams, and acceptance into a four-year college. Students as well as educational institutions are judged by this same system. Its pitfalls are brilliantly summed up with a letter written to the *Boston Globe* in 1991 by curriculum specialist Anita Teeter:

> Thousands of dollars are spent on this scam every year. The tests are counterproductive in that teachers concentrate on teaching test-taking, not on thinking skills. Teachers have known this for years, but they are under horrible stress because it is believed that the test results reflect on their teaching abilities and because their principals (also under stress to save their jobs and their schools) tell them to do whatever needs to be done to improve test scores. Principals are told the same thing by their superiors. The teachers I work with as a curriculum specialist are desperate.[1]

What would you think of a medical doctor who said to his patients, "Some of you are *A* and *B* patients and you really do not need a doctor, but I am going to give you a lot of attention and prescribe a medicine for you that will keep you well. Now, some individuals are *C* and *D* patients, and there are just so many of you I just can't give you much attention, even though several of you would do well with extra help. So what I'm going to do is to prescribe the *A* and *B* patient medicine for you and hope it will do you some good. Finally, some of you are *F* patients, and frankly that is just a part of life. Watch the *A* patients, take the same medicine they take, and who knows—some of you might improve. But I'm really not going to waste my time on someone that's going to die anyway.

No, that is not the way a good physician works. Instead, he or she will utilize the best diagnostic techniques and prescribe a health regimen and/or medicine that best applies to help each individual become healthy.

If that illustration does not fit well for you, let's try another. What about an instructor who is educating and training aircraft technicians. The aircraft industry cannot afford to have technicians who are *C* and *D* students, preparing airplanes for flight; their mistakes can be fatal! So the instructor aims at mastery of the material. Learning for understanding and for meaning is fundamental for any experiential technical education program. One can only wonder why learning for understanding and for mastery, at least mastery of the basics, has not caught on in the rest of education.

I am reminded of the school board member who exclaimed with tongue in cheek during a hot board discussion about the poor quality of education, "the trouble with our schools is that half of our students are below average." He was really trying to point out in a humorous way that schools are faced with the enormous assignment of educating all the kids with all of their diversity. But he was also protesting the meaninglessness of labels in describing individual students.

After reading the plethora of recommendations about improving American education, one might conclude that excellence in education can be achieved only by making the majority of students feel like failures. Anything other than a four-year university degree (or graduate degree) is viewed as somehow second rate. Anything other than a classical, theoretical curriculum is considered a compromise. And anyone not falling on the "smart" end of the bell curve is viewed as an embarrassment. As one high school student told me, "I was born dumb, and I guess that is my role in life!"

The trouble with that kind of thinking, however, is that it is dead wrong.

MORE THAN ONE KIND OF SMART

Much of the twentieth-century model of education has been built upon an understanding of intelligence represented by the standard IQ test, which measures only verbal and mathematical skills. But Howard Gardner, Director of Project Zero at the Harvard University Graduate School of Education, has concluded that the verbal/mathematical model of intelligence is much too narrow. He has theorized that there are at least *seven* different kinds of intelligences. Many teachers indicate that this view of intelligence has liberated them from the "one size fits all" pedagogy.

Gardner describes his seven different kinds of intelligence as follows:

1. *Intrapersonal intelligence* is the ability to form an accurate picture of oneself and to use that image to operate effectively in life.
2. *Interpersonal intelligence* is the ability to understand other people and to work cooperatively with them.
3. *Kinesthetic intelligence* is the ability to solve problems using all or parts of the body.
4. *Musical intelligence* is that ability to deal with rhythms and harmony, recognize tunes, and use various parts of the body to make music.
5. *Spatial intelligence* is the ability to form mental models of a spatial world. (Sculptors, engineers, surgeons, architects, and artists would exemplify this kind of intelligence.)
6. *Logical-mathematical intelligence* is the ability to analyze and solve problems following math and science principles.
7. *Linguistic intelligence* is the ability to recognize and use words and to create with words.[2]

Another prolific researcher/writer on the subject of intelligence is Robert Sternberg of Yale University. His 1988 book entitled *The Triarchic Mind; A New Theory of Human Intelligence*[3] also gives us new perspective into understanding intelligence. He posits that intelligence involves three elements:

1. *Componential intelligence,* which consists of the various cognitive processes (or components) required to carry out the adaptive behavior required by new situations—acquiring, retaining, retrieving, and translating information.

2. *Experiential intelligence*, the ability to solve new problems and adjust to new environments. The way an individual responds to the unusual or new gives an indication of this type of intelligence.

3. *Contextual intelligence*, a practical understanding of how to get along in the world.

The work on intelligence by Gardner, Sternberg, and others points to a significant conclusion: Unless we enlarge our definition of intelligence we

will continue to send the message that intelligence is a fixed capacity, that people either have it or don't, and that those who don't have it don't have much hope of any real success in school or in life.

A second-grade teacher's story provides a dramatic illustration that traditional ideas of intelligence fall far short. She was endeavoring to teach about commas, periods, and exclamation marks to a group of second graders who had been identified and labeled as *slow learners*. After repeated attempts to explain that a comma means slow down, a period means stop, and an exclamation mark mean emphasis the teacher could see no change in her students' reading; they continued to plow through the punctuation marks without understanding.

Exasperated, she had the students put on their wraps and follow her outside. She told them to walk in a circle while she read to them. She said, "When I say 'comma,' I want you to slow down. When I say 'period,' I want you to stop. When I say 'exclamation mark,' I want you to jump up and down." She tried this for several minutes, then led the students back into the classroom to read. And, each of them read much better—slowing at commas, stopping at periods, and giving emphasis at exclamation marks.

This illustration not only shows kinesthetic intelligence at work; it also gives us some insight into the dangers of writing off students who don't conform to our narrow standards of intelligence. In this and countless other cases, simply labeling children as "slow" on the basis of tests such as an IQ test did not help them learn. But varying the teaching method to suit their form of intelligence paid a big dividend in learning.[4]

Self-Fulfilling Prophecies

That such a belief can become a self-fulfilling prophecy is borne out by numerous studies. Almost without exception, these experiments lend credence to the theory that teachers and students tend to perform up to or down to expectations. One person's image of another person's intellectual ability can strongly influence performance.

One such experiment, described in Rosenthal and Jacobsen's *Pygmalion in the Classroom*,[5] revealed astonishing evidence that positive expectations of the teacher can be transferred to proud achievement, which in turn helps students develop a new image of their own intelligence.

The Pygmalion experiment was conducted in the Oak Elementary School, a public school serving a blue-collar community in a medium size city. The school followed the practice of "ability grouping" students—dividing them into fast, medium, and slow learners on the basis of a reading test.

At the beginning of the school year, each of the eighteen teachers in grades one through six was given the names of students who, because of their scores on a special new test, might be expected to demonstrate unusual academic growth. Actually, however, the students were chosen randomly. The only difference between them and other students was whatever difference existed in the mind of the teacher. The teachers were told to watch these students because they could be expected to bloom . . . and bloom they did!

IQ pre-tests and post-tests were administered to the experimental group and to a control group. After the first year of the experiment, 19 percent of the control group of students had gained twenty or more total IQ points, but *47 percent* of the experimental/expectancy group gained twenty or more points. Clearly, the students who were expected to improve lived up to expectations.

The Plight of the "Average" Child

It is especially important to note that the students placed in the medium (average) ability grouping made the greatest progress. These are individuals of the Neglected Majority—who have been more or less forgotten in school systems that focus all their attention and energy on students who make up the "smart" and the "challenged" ends of the traditional bell curve. The plight of the neglected "average" child was poignantly captured in this poem which a teacher sent me after I had given a speech in Wyoming. It was written by a ninth-grade Native American student who obviously knew the problem firsthand.

The Average Child
I don't cause teachers trouble,
my grades have been OK.
I listen in my classes
and I'm in school every day.

My teachers think I'm average,
my parents think so too.
I wish I didn't know that
'cause there's lots I'd like to do.

I'd like to build a rocket, I have
a book that tells you how,
or start a stamp collection—well
there's no use in trying now.

'Cause since I found I'm average
I'm just smart enough you see,
to know there is nothing special
that I should expect of me.

I'm part of the majority,
that hump part of the bell,
who spends their life unnoticed
in an average kind of hell.[6]

It is time for all of us in the United States culture to recognize the many kinds of human intelligence and to nurture student abilities in all of their diverse dimensions. When that happens, overall academic performance cannot help but improve.

Excellence in education will never be found by sorting and labeling students according to IQ, grades, test scores, or any other device. It will not even be found by seeking out and adopting a few new teaching techniques. Excellence will be developed as all teachers begin to understand the diversity of human ability, the incredible power of the human brain, and the effectiveness of an application-oriented, learner-centered educational strategy. An IQ score or a placement on a bell curve must not be allowed to limit a student's possibilities.

BARRIERS TO EXCELLENCE

I am convinced that educational excellence is a worthy and achievable goal for every student, every school. However, a number of faulty ideas and unsound practices stand in the way of cultivating excellence throughout our schools. In the remainder of this chapter I want to examine each of these in turn. My hope is that recognizing these barriers will be the first step toward eliminating them altogether.

Barrier #1: Faulty Images of Excellence

There is little agreement among educational leaders (or anyone else, for that matter) about the definition of excellence in education. Most of us base our understanding of excellence on unexamined assumptions and mental images that may not match reality.

What is the typical image of educational excellence? It is that of "smart kids" who perform well on verbal or mathematical kinds of tests and who make good grades in English, math, and other traditional subjects. These stereotypical models of excellence then go on to attend a four-year college, where they also excel in traditional subjects, make good grades, perhaps go to graduate school, and then enter a profession such as law, medicine—or education.

The reality, of course, is that this is a reasonable scenario for a relatively small minority of students—those whose intelligence leans toward the linguistic or the mathematical, those who learn well in the theoretical or abstract mode, those who *want* to got to the university and be lawyers, doctors, accountants, engineers, teachers and the like. But this is simply not the likeliest—or the best—scenario for all students, or even the majority of students.

The 1990 census reveals, for instance, that about 20 percent of the American population twenty-five years of age or older actually hold a four-year-college-baccalaureate degree. Even given a dramatic growth of baccalaureate-degree holders over this next decade, at least three out of four students in the public schools will not likely earn a college baccalaureate degree. Are we prepared to write off this large majority simply because our image of excellence is too narrow?

A pervasive but unrealistic and limited image of excellence in education has led parents, teachers, educational leaders, and even students to say that some individuals *can't learn* (and therefore cannot achieve excellence in education). Some even attempt to support this view on the basis of genetic differences that limit the learning capacity of some students.

But there is now considerable evidence indicating that most of us use only a small portion of the full capacity of our cerebrum, the large "thinking brain" that is the seat of mental consciousness and the learner's most valuable tool. And herein lies a conundrum: If we still do not know the full capacity of the brain to learn, how can anyone state as a fact that some students can't learn? We would be closer to the truth if we said that some students have trouble learning when presented with only theoretical and abstract teaching methodologies and materials. Perhaps the major difference between those we label as academically talented and all the others rests in their abilities (and willingness) to tolerate a teaching-learning situation that is neither motivating nor effective.

The educational community is not alone, of course, in forming unrealistic images of excellence. Madison Avenue has developed an advertising image of excellence based upon a thin, attractive, moderately young family living confident and happy in a meticulously landscaped and spacious suburban home. Each morning, after a breakfast which builds bodies in twelve ways, two children skip off to the neighborhood school. Presumably, within the standardized time of nine months times twelve years they will graduate from high school in the above average half of their class. Then, with little effort, they will continue their education at a prestigious university. Unfortunately, this unreal image of excellence has sunk deep into the American culture and therefore has spilled over into the schools. Teachers and students are not immune to the cultural views of our society—even when those views are based on unreal images.

The television and movie industry portrays another faulty image of excellence that directly affects our assessment of educational excellence. The multimillionaire athlete, movie star, or rock star becomes a powerful if unattainable role model. These folks often have a much stronger influence upon student values than teachers, or sometimes even parents. Reading, writing, and arithmetic become incidental also-runs to the more dramatic skills of a professional athlete or a rock star. The media image of excellence tends to stress form over substance. The photo opportunity becomes more important than the message. How someone looks becomes more important than what he or she says. Clearly, any of these assumptions has the power to change how we view excellence in education.

TABLE 1
WHAT IS AN EXCELLENT EDUCATION? IMAGE VS. REALITIES

UNREAL EDUCATIONAL IMAGES	EDUCATIONAL REALITIES
One classical school curriculum will meet the needs of all students.	Students need structure and substance in their school programs, but presented in context so they can see the application of their learning.
All students learn at approximately the same rate of speed.	There are vast individual differences among students of any age in speed of learning and comprehension of knowledge.
All students must learn the basic completion skills by the elementary grades.	Development of basic skills must be placed upon a continuum of learning, with students arriving at different points at different times. Excellence in education requires breaking the lockstep of arbitrary time requirements for learning.
The traditional classical textbook and lecture method of instruction is the most effective approach to teaching for most students.	Some students learn rapidly by one method of instruction and more slowly under a different approach. However, contextual teaching-learning appears consistently more effective than classical instruction.
Real excellence can be found only among those students and programs related to the pursuance of a college baccalaureate degree.	Some new definitions of excellence are needed. Excellence is just as important to the aircraft technician as to the engineer, to the secretary as to the business professor. Every school and college program must develop standards of excellence, and the goal of excellence must be held up for every course and each student.
Covering the subject-matter material is more important than gaining a depth of understanding. Education becomes a mile wide and an inch deep.	Depth is more important than breadth in helping students gain understanding. Instead of concentrating on covering the textbook, teachers should select and choose material to help students understand the application of knowledge.

In some institutions of higher education, the definition of excellence begins with the admissions process. "Who gets in?" becomes the key question Such institutions seem to assume that educational excellence will be ensured if the entrance screening process is thorough enough in sorting the so-called academically talented from the not-so-talented. But does such a policy really foster excellence—or does it simply maintain a system for sifting and sorting out students who vary from the accepted image?

There is nothing inherently wrong with tough program admission standards as long as they are not viewed as the only key to achieving educational excellence. But the open door public schools and community colleges must work on the basis of a not-so-visible definition of excellence. Certainly these schools want well-prepared entering students; however they must recognize there are several kinds of intelligence and therefore several definitions of excellence. They cannot achieve excellence by screening out students, but most focus instead upon "value-added excellence" or academic progress. They must ask, "Where was this student upon entry and how well has he or she progressed?

Barrier #2: A Diverse Population

The continual national thrashing around about how to "fix" education underscores the still-experimental nature of the American education enterprise. We still have not discovered the methodology to meet the needs of the sheer diversity of individuals attending our schools and colleges. Anyone who has spent much time in a public-school classroom can attest to the awesome array of individual differences among the students.

One of the most pressing dilemmas for educators is to develop a working criterion of excellence that fits the great range of individual differences among students—whether rich or poor, black or white, able or "challenged," or destined for the university, community college, apprenticeship, or a specific job, including homemaking. The varieties of student aspirations and the multiplicity of socioeconomic and cultural backgrounds and experiences require multiple pedagogical approaches, but all students must have an equal opportunity for excellence. To that end, we must learn to ignore the shibboleth that the traditional college prep-baccalaureate degree program is the only road to excellence, respect, and dignity.

Social and educational status must not be allowed to substitute for equality of opportunity and individual achievement regardless of the curriculum or the field of study. It will be a sorrowful day indeed if the "pursuit of excellence" becomes a cover for a retreat from equity and opportunity concerns. Elitism cannot become a substitute for excellence.

Clearly, American education requires a new definition of excellence in education, a definition that will hold meaning for all students rather than just some of them. It is time for the varieties of excellence to which we aspire in our universal education system to match the sheer diversity of our students. Educational excellence simply cannot be achieved by providing the same educational experiences and the same time frame for learning for everyone. An educational institution that provides the same pedagogical approach, the same resources, and the same time for learning for all students cannot truly make the claim of cultivating excellence.

Barrier #3: "High Standards"

One concerned high school principal recently related to me that more than four hundred of his twelve hundred students had received one or more failing grades during the fall semester of the 1992 school year. In his musing upon this observation, he wondered if the students were at fault . . . or if the school was doing something wrong. His next comment was telling:

> We are trying to pursue excellence in this high school. We have high expectations, tough courses, and high standards. We are proud of how many students we place into good colleges and of our large number of merit scholarship winners each year. I guess we just cannot expect our average students to do well in our higher-level academic courses.[7]

This principal was ignoring, along with many of his colleagues, the fact that having "high standards" is only half the solution. The more important half is *designing programs that help students meet those high standards*.

There are at least three ways to help students meet high standards.

First, we can give all students the same curriculum and fail those who do not memorize well or think well in the abstract, who are not eighteen-week learners (one semester), or who simply fail to see the point in what they are asked to learn. This remains the option of choice in many schools and colleges.

Second, we can "dumb down" the curriculum and make it easy enough for all to succeed. Instead of reexamining our pedagogical methods, we just water down the content and grade more leniently. The students' mental "toolboxes" are filled with fluff and the inconsequential rather than the tools for lifelong learning.

Or third, we can examine our teaching and consider whether we are teaching for meaning, for connectedness. We can consider whether we are helping students see the application of knowledge. Rather than dumbing down the content, we can teach differently using the LogoLearning process of content, context, assimilation, and problem solving.

Clearly, the third option, the LogoLearning option, makes more sense. When we make the effort to teach for meaning, we help all students reach high standards and open the door to excellence for everyone.

Barrier #4: Fragmentation

One of the most serious barriers to educational excellence has already been mentioned several times in this book; it is program fragmentation. Students are expected to go from class to class, subject to subject, even from grade to grade and school to school with little sense of connection or continuity. For the most part, it is left up to the student to grasp that the use of mathematical formulas might be helpful in a graphic-arts class or that English lessons in clear communication might apply to answering an essay question in history. And other than being told that some classes have "prerequisites" and certain subjects must be completed for graduation, most students have little sense that one class is building on another—or preparing them for much of anything that connects.

As a result, the majority of students experience an unfocused "general education" that relates to little, leads to little, and prepares for little. This kind of fragmented learning is rarely effective in motivating students or building personal confidence and competence. It certainly does not promote excellence.

One of the important lessons yet to be learned by many educators is that the "why" of learning is as important as the "how"—and that "why" issues must be addressed *before* the "how" issues. Human beings live best by living on our hopes rather than our fears, by looking to the future. Those students who fail to see the purpose of their education also often see no point in even continuing school, much less striving for excellence.

One of the disappointing aspects of the major reports on education reform in recent years is the scant attention given to continuity in learning. Fred Hechinger, long-time observer of the American educational scene comments:

> We are not very good at continuity.... As a result of that, American education during the past few decades has become a collection of disjointed parts that in the main fail to connect. . . . The lack of continuity that plagues American education is something that all of education needs to address. Instead of connecting the separate levels, critics generally compound the spirit of separation by seeking scapegoats instead of remedies. . . .
> If we want to reform the schools, two things are essential: continuity, all the way up the line; and understanding the "why" of every single course. Read Bruno Bettleheim on that. Whatever you teach, make the children understand why they are studying it. Don't tell them: "You'll need it later." *Later doesn't exist.*[8]

The tremendous mobility of contemporary American society contributes to the chronic lack of continuity in learning. An estimated 25 percent of public-school students attend more than one public school each year. Given this reality, it is amazing that some students learn as much as they do.

Irregular class attendance also contributes to lack of continuity. It's hard for students to feel a sense of connectedness from one class to another when they miss a significant number of their classes. It is a fairly safe bet that overall student achievement would improve dramatically in most schools if student class attendance patterns improved.

It is true that schools have little control over some of these factors. Certainly schools cannot (nor should not) force parents not to move, and schools have only limited power to force students to attend classes. But I am convinced that schools can do a better job of helping students make up for time lost in transition or in absence. For example, as I mentioned in chapter 2, self-learning laboratories could provide students with the opportunity to catch up in areas where they fall behind; this approach might even be an excellent way to connect public libraries more closely with the other educational institutions. Recent advances in technology have made such labs increasingly feasible.

Another loss of continuity happens between high schools and colleges. For some students this gap must seem like crossing the Grand Canyon, when it should simply be a gateway to a continued learning experience. Some of this loss of continuity can be attributed to the widely decentralized nature of our educational system, which inhibits communication. Opening the lines of educational communication will take much effort, but they must be opened if continuity in learning is to be achieved.

Barrier #5: Misuse of Tests

Yet another significant barrier to excellence in education is the misuse of intelligence and achievement tests. We are only now beginning to understand the extent to which the traditional use of these multiple-choice, computer-graded instruments has hindered the cultivation of excellence in our schools and colleges. In this understanding we are indebted to scholars such as Howard Gardner, with his theory of multiple intelligences, and Stephen Gould, with his valuable work on the misuse of tests. Gardner himself sums it up beautifully:

> We should spend less time ranking children and more time helping them to identify their natural competencies and gifts and cultivate those. There are hundreds and hundreds of ways to succeed and many, many different abilities that will help you get there.[9]

The testing movement, by and large, defies rational observation about how individuals learn and how effective education works. In fact, the word *test* has become a four letter word for many teachers.

IQ tests, for example, which were developed to predict success or failure in school, were based upon a philosophy that each individual has a finite amount of intelligence. A few individuals have high intelligence, the theory goes, but the vast majority are of average or below average intellectual abilities—hence the bell-shaped curve. As we have seen, several decades of study as well as the experience of most teachers refute that misconception. Yet IQ tests continue to be used as a means of labeling and sorting students in too many cases.

It is interesting to note that scores for standardized achievement tests such as the ACT (American College Test) or SAT (Scholastic Aptitude Test), both widely used as criteria for college admissions, follow an almost identical bell-shaped curve as do IQ tests. Almost without exception, such tests provide few ways of evaluating whether students can solve problems, apply knowledge, see things in the mind's eye—all vital skills both for ongoing education and for success in the larger world.

And yet despite the obvious deficiencies of standardized testing as a means of assessment, the pressure is on to test more, not less. The rhetoric has gushed from a wide array of political leaders that Americans are being shortchanged in the education product. Education is costing more and achieving less, they say; educational institutions must be held accountable; and the way to do that is to measure how students score on standardized tests. Schools and school systems are being judged on the basis of arbitrary grade-level achievement tests. Scores from these tests are even compared with expenditures to arrive at some judgment of cost effectiveness.

TABLE 2
AVERAGE SAT SCORES IN LOWEST- AND HIGHEST-SPENDING STATES[10]

State	School Expenditures Per Pupil 1989-1990	Average SAT Score 1990	Percent of H.S. Seniors Taking SAT 1990
Lowest-Spending States			
Utah	$2,817	1031	5%
Mississippi	3,119	996	4%
Arkansas	3,185	981	6%
Idaho	3,195	968	17%
Alabama	3,321	984	8%
Average	$3,127	992	5%
Highest-Spending States			
Rhode Island	$6,425	883	62%
Alaska	7,816	914	42%
Connecticut	7,869	901	74%
New York	7,946	882	70%
New Jersey	8,439	891	69%
Average	$7,699	894	63%

On the surface, test scores and expenditure levels sound like a reasonable basis for judging the quality and cost-effectiveness of our national investment in education. The media and the public are demanding some simple and understandable basis for making judgments about educational quality. This has resulted in a "push-button accountability" response from political leaders.

There can be no question that educators must be accountable for their efforts and the wise use of public funds. But let's dig deeper in utilizing test scores before make accountability judgments.

Some political leaders are quick to point out, for instance, that students are scoring higher on the Scholastic Aptitude Test in low-spending states than in higher-spending states. What they overlook is the number of students taking this test. An examination of the statistics found in table 2 reveals that in a low per-student expenditure state such as Utah, only 5 percent of the high school seniors took the SAT. At the same time, in a high per-student expenditure state such as Connecticut, some 74 percent, or nearly three out of four, of seniors took the SAT.

A ten-year study (1982 to 1992) of ACT and SAT test results reveals that average overall scores have remained fairly constant, with a point up or point down here and there. Yet, the number of individuals taking the ACT and SAT tests over the same ten-year period has nearly doubled, and this with a declining school enrollment. What has obviously happened is that the ranks of test takers have expanded to include the middle 50 percent of high school students as well as the top academic quartile. When considering the fact that many more students are now taking the college entrance exams, stable test scores may be a sign of progress and not of stagnation. Given the larger pool of test takers, educators have had to work harder just to maintain the same average test scores year after year.

Of course, this analysis will not satisfy many of those convinced that all students should be measured by the same yardstick. It does suggest an interesting possibility, however. If we are going to continue making judgments about educational quality on the basis of college entrance exams, which measure primarily theoretical verbal/mathematical abilities, then why not just limit the pool of test takers to the top academic 25 percent of our high school student bodies, as is the case in many other countries? Test scores will likely rise dramatically if we do so. Political leaders can be proud of their efforts to improve the quality of education. The media can report that schools and colleges are making great educational improvements.

But the key question will remain, of course: Will this type of testing and misuse of testing outcomes really improve the educational product? Clearly, the answer is no.

Let there be no doubt that educators must continue to work hard at improving the quality of education at all levels of schools, community colleges, and universities. We must strive for excellence at all levels of the educational endeavor. But as we have seen, standardized tests have little to do with educational excellence for the majority of students. In fact, there is strong evidence that tests and the process of preparing for them are actually counterproductive to excellence.

A 1991 study conducted by Lorrie Shepard and colleagues at the University of Colorado, for example, revealed that student test scores dropped dramatically when students at thirty-six schools were retested a few weeks after they took the required standardized tests. Shepard concluded that standardized test preparations consist almost entirely of rote memorization and that the actual material covered makes little impression on the students; it is quickly lost after the test is over.

Shepard's conclusion is borne out by a simple comparison of student test scores at various times. For example, some two thirds of Indiana's eighth graders outscored the national average on the California Achievement Tests in 1988, but only 14 percent had mastered even seventh-grade skills on a similar federally funded exam two years later. In Virginia, 56 percent of eighth graders scored above the national average on the Iowa Tests of Basic Skills in 1989. But on a similar federally funded test given one year later, only 15 percent could achieve the same level of mastery.

Not only is the standardized testing movement not giving us a true assessment of excellence in teaching and learning, but also it is expensive and time consuming. A study by Mary Lee Smith at Arizona State University revealed that the nation's elementary teachers spend an average of three to four weeks in preparation for the standardized tests—time that could be used in far more effective ways.

Reading and writing are taught more effectively by having students read and write about meaningful things than by memorizing and writing lists of unrelated words. Skill drill alone is boring for student and teacher, particularly when we know that students learn best when skills are taught within the context of use. Preparing students for some arbitrary test through meaningless workbook exercises does little to further the cause of excellence in education.[11]

So why do we test? If students do not retain the material they memorize in preparing for the tests, if preparation eats up money and classroom time, and if standardized tests do not tell us much about overall educational quality, one can only wonder why we continue this practice.

Fortunately, however, there seems to be hope for the testing movement. Instruments and methods are being developed that end the tyranny of the "multiple guess" and provide for more authentic means of assessment. The American College Testing Service, for example, has now developed a new testing program called Work Keys which combines testing for knowing with testing for doing. Another promising possibility is the trend toward the development of student portfolios that demonstrate accomplishment through a demonstration of student work—essays, lab experiments, problem-solving exercises, writing tests, and math exams based on open-ended problems. Authentic assessment practices, particularly the use of student portfolios, are now in place in about half the states, and the state of Vermont is providing leadership in the movement toward more authentic assessment and portfolio development.

Authentic assessment is an attractive alternative to the traditional standardized testing program. We must keep in mind, however, that much of the impetus for testing comes from political, not educational sources. Progress in this area, therefore, does not answer the political questions about institutional accountability. If the standardized-testing approach is to be avoided, educators must come up with other performance indicators that will give the public a clear sense of educational quality and accountability. Otherwise it will just be too easy to keep students filling in the answer bubbles on the multiple-choice tests and continue to make erroneous judgments about the quality of work going on in a school or college.

Barrier #6: Too Much to Cover!

There are many other barriers to excellence that I don't have space to cover—the lack of an adequate staff-development program, for example, or the serious problem of anemic school financing. In concluding this chapter on the search for excellence, however, I feel I must address an important issue that is rarely discussed. It involves the sheer amount of curricular material that teachers and students are expected to cover.

It is the textbooks that usually determine the content of a given course of study. And most modern textbook publishers seem to operate upon the theory that more is always better. Material is often constantly added in the interest of timeliness, but seldom is older material deleted to make room for the additions. As a consequence, many textbooks are so packed with facts, details, names, and places that they read like the venerable and voluminous— but now-defunct—Sears catalog!

Exposing students to more material does not mean they will learn more. More likely, attempting to "cover the material" in a packed curriculum usually means that the students receive only a superficial exposure to a massive amount of information and learn nothing in depth. LogoLearning advocates moving away from the "more is better" theory in curriculum building, teaching, and learning, toward a theory of "go deeper rather than wider."

The textbooks published by U.S. publishers cover more material than textbooks from any other country. The science textbooks in Pacific Rim countries, for example, focus on less material but teach it in far greater depth than the information-laden texts in the United States.[12] One can only wonder if the oft-cited differences between the quality of Pacific Rim education and that of U.S. education have anything to do with this issue of depth versus breadth.

In many U.S. schools today, particularly elementary and secondary schools, much of the information to which students are exposed tends to become dormant knowledge or what Alfred North Whitehead calls "inert knowledge."[13] This is information that the student remembers hearing or seeing or even memorizing, but that holds little meaning and that the student never actually uses. Such information, I would suggest, is practically worthless.

Wouldn't it be much better to present less information but to present it in ways that allow for in-depth learning. If students are to truly master a subject, they must be able to do more than simply hear it or even memorize it. They must be provided with appropriate experiences that enable them to make connections between the information and what it means.

The simple textbooks published over a hundred years ago in the United States were probably better at helping students connect subject-matter content with context than the textbooks of today. The earlier texts, of course, were not required to deal with as tremendous a volume of information as today. But, there was something salutary about the limited information these texts offered. It allowed the teacher to go into greater depth and provide the student with related experiences. Note for example the introductory statement to teachers in *Swinton's Third Reader*, published in 1882:

In the selection, adaptation, and composition of the reading-pieces, the most earnest effort has been put forth to furnish sound and sweet mental food. An attempt has also been made to introduce into the book a little of what may be called organism (experience) by carrying on a certain number of pieces on distinct strains, a series of lessons on 'Home Pets,' as the living forms most familiar and interesting to children; a second series, 'Bright Examples,' to touch and stimulate the affections; and a third series, 'About Plants,' as a slight glimpse of Nature in one of her most attractive aspects.[14]

The major objective of LogoLearning is to find ways to help students connect knowledge with the touchstones of reality and experience that are as complex and challenging as real life. This kind of teaching takes time because experiences must be processed and pondered. As a result, connections will be made that provide in-depth understanding and help the student assimilate this knowledge for future problem solving.

I believe it is time for educators to begin the process of winnowing and reducing their curricula. The message must go forth to textbook publishers, school boards, school administrators, and all who control the curriculum that enough is enough. Coverage of material for the sake of coverage will simply not produce excellence in learning. If we are seriously interested in excellence, the curriculum must be reduced, and teachers must be encouraged to deemphasize breadth in favor of subject-matter depth. We can no longer allow the education curricula to be a mile wide and an inch deep.

A question may arise in this regard: Isn't there a standard and growing body of information (knowledge) that all students in a given society should be expected to master? The answer to this question is yes, but only as related to the agreed-upon purposes of education (for a fuller discussion of educational purposes, see chapter 2). We must also remind ourselves that contemporary students gain information from many sources, particularly from that intrusive teacher called television. Educational institutions are no longer the only major player in furnishing information. However, they *should* be the major player in helping students to understand the application of knowledge and to connect that knowledge with meaning that will enable them to solve problems in new situations.

TOWARD A NEW UNDERSTANDING OF EXCELLENCE

The information age, sped by rapid technological advances, presents a richer but more complex reality for educators at all levels. It just may be easier to create an information-age society than to maintain one. In other words, we know more about job placement than job creation, more about training than retraining, and more about excellence in some aspects of education than others. Frankly, we need to come up with some new models of excellence that correspond to the needs of students and society in a rapidly changing culture. This means we must face up to the barriers that often stand in the way of excellence—barriers such as faulty assumptions about what excellence means, the need to educate a diverse population, "high standards" that are not linked to student enablement, fragmented curricula, the misuse of tests, and the need to cover too much material. LogoLearning offers hope for removing or at least reducing some of these barriers.

Excellence in teaching and learning cannot be pursued as though chasing an elusive butterfly. It certainly cannot be achieved simply by sorting and labeling students. Excellence will happen only as we nourish and cultivate the educational soil with some new pedagogical approaches so that students of all races, genders, and cultural backgrounds can grow and mature. True excellence in education must be excellence that is achievable for everyone.

[1] Evans Clinchy, "Needed: A Clinton Crusade for Quality and Equality," *Phi Delta Kappan,* April 1993, 607.

[2] For more information see Howard Gardner, *Frames of Mind: The Theory of Multiple Intelligence* (New York: Basic Books, 1983) and Gardner's tenth anniversary edition of *Frames of Mind* (New York: Basic Books, 1992). See also Gardner, *The Unschooled Mind* (New York: Basic Books, 1991) and "Beyond the IQ: Education and Human Development," *Phi Kappa Phi Journal,* Spring 1988.

[3] Robert Sternberg, *The Triarchic Mind; A New Theory of Human Intelligence* (New York: Viking, 1988).

[4] This story was first presented in Renate Nummela and Geoffrey Caine, *Making Connections: Teaching and the Human Brain* (Alexandria: Association for Supervision and Curriculum Development, 1991), 109.

[5] Robert Rosenthal and Lenore Jacobsen, *Pygmalion in the Classroom* (New York: Holt, Rinehart and Winston, 1968, 1992).

[6] Ninth-grade Native American student, name withheld by request.

[7] Name and school withheld upon request.

[8] Fred M. Hechinger, "School-College Collaboration—An Essential to Improved Public Education," *National Association of Secondary School Principals Bulletin,* October 1984, 69–79.

[9] Howard Gardner, quoted in David Goleman, "Rethinking the Value of Intelligence Tests," *New York Times Supplement,* 9 November 1986, 2.

[10] Source: National Education Association, U. S. Department of Education.

[11] There is a distinctive difference between "teaching for the test," in the sense that student purposes and objectives are established up front (see chapter 3), and simply drilling students so that they can do well on a standardized test.

[12] Frank Dempster, "Exposing Our Students to Less Should Help Them Learn More," *Phi Delta Kappan,* February 1993, 433–437.

[13] Alfred North Whitehead, *Process and Reality* (New York: Free Press, 1979).

[14] *Swinton's Third Grade Readers* (New York: American Book Company, 1882).

CHAPTER 5

A Right-Side-Up Education

Putting First Things First

I hear and I forget.
I see and I remember.
I do and I understand.

–Old Chinese Proverb

*I*s it a puzzle? Normally, we cannot get to the second things by putting them first. We can secure the second things only by putting first things first. Yet in so many American classrooms we are putting second things first! We are trying to lead students from theory to practice, from the unreal to the real, from the unknown to the known, from the unfamiliar to the familiar—despite the evidence that for most students that approach to teaching and learning is simply not effective.

LogoLearning turns that kind of learning upside down—or, rather, right side up. It insists that we give priority to understanding over memorization, active problem solving over passive learning, connected knowing over segregated knowledge. It requires that we spark a spirit of discovery in students rather than simply telling them about other individuals' discoveries. It takes exception to a system that isolates schools and colleges from real-world experiences and that provides students with knowledge without empowering them to apply that knowledge in important, practical ways.

And right-side-up education is revolutionary. LogoLearning reform is not satisfied with making a few marginal changes in the teaching-learning process. Instead, it calls for a thoughtful reexamination of what we believe about how we teach, how students learn, and what our purpose is in doing both.

A RIGHT-SIDE-UP VIEW OF THE CONTENT-VERSUS-CONTEXT DEBATE

In much of our ongoing discussion and debate about improving education, most participants seem to be hung up on one of two divergent philosophical positions:

- *Content philosophy:* learning to know is most important; application can come later.
- *Context philosophy:* learning to do is most important, and knowledge will somehow seep into the process.

Much of the current "how to fix it" discussion springs from the split between these two differing philosophies. To illustrate this divergence, let's look at recent efforts to develop federal education reform.

In 1993 the Clinton administration developed and presented to Congress a reform package called Goals 2000. This legislation, which consisted of House Resolution 3120 and Senate Bill 1150, covered a number of interrelated educational issues. First, it proposed a set of national educational goals, which as I explained in chapter 2 were actually anticipated outcome statements. Second, it authorized certification of national content standards (subjects and facts students would be required to master) and assessments based upon these content standards. Third, it proposed opportunity-to-learn standards, which are statements about the educational practices required in order for students to properly learn the subject matter. Finally, the legislation authorized the development of national job-skill standards and created a program of grants to assist states with their related education reform efforts.

What I found interesting about the development of this new omnibus national education reform legislation was the differences that developed between the Senate and House versions of this legislation, as well as the debate that ensued among various congressional leaders about the issue of content versus context. The Senate version stressed content as the primary concern of educational endeavors and remained silent on context and teaching methods. The House version indicated that there must be a connection between content standards and opportunity-to-learn standards—that what is taught should be connected with how it is taught. The leaders of the House Labor and Education Committee made it clear in the congressional debates that they would approve of the content standards only if the states receiving grants from the federal appropriation would guarantee that opportunity-to-learn standards would also be implemented.

This classic debate among politicians only illustrates the depth of disagreement among Americans about the purposes of education and the relationship between content and context. And the cause of better education loses if either side "wins."

If we stress only the content direction, then we should drop the word *reform* from our educational and political jargon because this approach appears to only promote more of traditional subject-matter disciplines, dressed up a bit. On the other hand, if we stress only the context direction as being most important, then we should drop the word *education* from our discussions and just talk about training.

We must move off of dead center in these discussions. Content and context are *both* important; you can't have one without the other. The most effective education—the LogoLearning education—is one that consistently teaches content by means of contextual examples and that imbues contextual activities with solid content.

EDUCATIONAL ISOLATIONISM

We live in an interdependent and interconnected world. Students must be given the opportunity to understand the nature of that interconnectedness and to explore how our contemporary culture and economy operate, warts and all. LogoLearning aims at breaking through the long-standing isolation of schools and colleges from the world all around them. Indeed, the LogoLearning teaching-learning process aims to serve as a bridge between the classroom and the real world. Let us look at a few examples of education isolationism.

Example #1: Who Pays for Schools?

It is a sad irony that after twelve years of schooling (and sometimes even after sixteen years), most students who attended public institutions have no idea how their schooling was financed. Who paid the education tax bills and why? How are schools and colleges governed? What is meant by an ad valorem tax? No wonder that public schools and colleges have difficulty gaining adequate financial support! The individuals being served by education have never been exposed to the question of who pays for their education . . . and why?

Example #2: What Does It Mean to Be a Citizen?

How many students graduating from schools and colleges today know much about the Oath of American Citizenship?

> I hereby declare, on oath, that I absolutely and entirely renounce and adjure all allegiance and fidelity to any foreign prince, poten-tate, state, or sovereignty of whom or which I have heretofore been a subject or citizen; that I will support and defend the Constitution and laws of the United States of America against all enemies, foreign and domestic; that I will bear true faith and allegiance to the same; that I will bear arms on behalf of the United States when required by law; that I will perform work of national importance under civilian direction when required by law; and that I will take this obligation freely without any mental reservation or purpose of evasion; so help me God.

With this oath, individuals seeking United States citizenship pledge to support our federal Constitution. They *know* what it means to be a citizen. Unfortunately, native-born U.S. citizens often take our constitutional rights and responsibilities for granted. It is sad but true that most *new* U.S. citizens have a better understanding of what it means to be a citizen than most native-born Americans do.

The health and vigor or our democracy depend in large measure upon the ability of our schools and colleges to transmit to each new generation the political vision of liberty, equality, and responsibility that unites our nation. This vision must go beyond knowledge to commitment and application—not a knee-jerk patriotism, but a deeply felt commitment based upon factual knowledge and understanding that have been critically analyzed. Education should make a difference not only in the intellectual and practical competence of students, but also in the level of civic responsibility they are willing to shoulder. Yet we must ask if education is achieving that high goal.

An "attitude" study of American youth commissioned by People for the American Way and conducted by Peter Hart Research Associates in 1989 provided a detailed look at the values and goals of young people (aged fifteen through twenty-four), at their ideas about citizenship and their interest in civic learning. The survey results were discouraging. When students were asked to describe a good citizen, for example, only 12 percent of those surveyed volunteered voting as a basic characteristic. In reviewing the overall results of the study, Arthur J. Kropp, president of People for the American Way, commented:

> This study sounds the alarm for America's democracy. It paints a troubling portrait of a generation that is for very understandable reasons turned off and tuning out to politics and citizen participation. . . . Politicians, the media and all Americans need to take a good look at our failure to get our young people thinking positively about our political process. Our neglect is chipping away at the very foundation of our democracy: our next generation's preparedness to take on the awesome task of self-government.[1]

Example #3: What About Cars?

Let's look at the automobile as another example of the pervasive discrepancy between schooling and the real world. The automobile has a profound impact not only on the economy of our country and on our personal finances, but on our very lives. In any given year, between forty-six to fifty thousand individuals are killed in motor vehicle accidents across the country, yet in most schools, any form of driver education, including driver safety, is considered a frill. An estimated 181 million cars, trucks, buses, and motorcycles are registered in the United States, yet school curricula rarely address these vehicles' impact on demographic, economic, or environmental conditions. The U.S. government estimates that owning and operating the average vehicle now costs more than four thousand dollars per year, yet there is little room in the school curricula for studying the way that owning a car may impact our personal finances.

For that matter, the typical high school student has little to say about the management of personal finances, auto loans, home mortgages, health insurance, and many of the financial issues that impact the lives of us all. More than a half-million bankruptcies are filed across the country each year, but it is a challenge to find discussion of this important economic issue in the typical school curriculum.

Example #4: Is It Ever too Late to Learn the Basics?

If there is one thing at which schools and colleges should excel, it is in helping individuals develop the competencies to function as lifelong learners. What are these competencies? Here is a skeletal list: reading speed and comprehension skills, listening and speaking skills, analytical skills, problem-solving skills, decision-making skills, synthesizing skills, human relation skills, computational skills, and, more recently, computer skills.

Ideally, of course, students would begin developing these competencies very early in their schooling and would continue to build on them throughout their educational career. But what if something goes wrong? What if illness or absences or emotional problems or frequent moves prevent a student from getting a good start in the basics? Or what if students or even adults would simply like to increase their skills in certain areas? (Many adults, for instance, would like to increase their reading speed and comprehension, yet they certainly do not regard themselves as remedial students.)

According to current educational practice, an individual who has not developed these competencies to a certain level by the end of the eighth grade is more or less doomed to educational purgatory, at least in high school. How many arbitrary barriers have been developed to prevent such individuals from developing lifelong-learner skills? Where is the curricular home in the average secondary school to help individuals develop the competencies that will enable them to be an effective life-long learner?

A number of community colleges have established developmental education programs (sometimes called college preparatory programs) to address these needs. But, even they have had to overcome the protests of legislators, academicians, and those who say these skills should have been learned much earlier. Some state and federal college financing schemes actually mitigate against helping postsecondary students develop their lifelong learner needs by saying that adults who have not acquired the necessary college-going competencies are ineligible for student financial aid.

Example #5: Doesn't What I've Learned Outside of School Count for Something?

In many ways learning has leaped the boundaries of schools and colleges. Employers and community-based organizations are offering more and more learning opportunities to employees and citizens. Every year, for example, an estimated half-million adults earn their high-school diplomas via the General Education Development (GED) testing program. At the same time, an estimated million adults across the nation earn college credits via extra-institutional channels. A growing number of adults are earning college credits for learning acquired in the military, or on the job, or through telecourses. An increasing number of adults are seeking out private training centers of various kinds just to upgrade their skills.

Yet, some schools and colleges seem oblivious to this phenomenon and actually establish barriers to make it difficult to earn credits in the extra-institutional manner. In terms of the transfer of college credits by students from one institution to another (particularly between community colleges and four-year colleges), one can only wonder at the logic involved. What is the rationale for allowing the transfer of credits for a course such as tennis but denying the transfer of credit for a course such as electronics? With little effort one could find hundreds of similar illustrations that seem to defy rational logic. It may be a tongue-in-cheek observation, but one could almost conclude that a student may transfer college credits from a community college to a university only if they are not useful. Any subject matter that smacks of being practical and useful cannot possibly be allowed as a transfer credit.

This statement must not be misunderstood. Certainly there are training courses that would not be appropriate for university transfer status, but many others are appropriate. An increasing number of university and community college educators are in almost continuous dialogue about this issue. My plea is simply to urge the reexamination of the logic behind the decisions about what courses are transferable.

The contemporary system of education has not come to grips with the complexity and turbulence engendered by an amazing increase of information and the wrenching shift in the nature of work. Without developing some new ways of thinking about human intelligence and the teaching-learning process, the formal education institutions will only become less and less productive and responsive. For example, it is becoming a self-defeating endeavor for any one person to keep up with the ever-multiplying flow of information. For this reason, the focus of education must be not imparting information to students, but helping them learn where to find and how to analyze information.

Example #6: Does Work Count?

The majority of today's high school students have jobs. It is estimated that two-thirds to three-fourths of the high school students today work at a paying job at some time during their high school experience, but the schools rarely seem to recognize this fact. In fact, much of the discussion in the 1990s about school-to-work transition, work-based learning, and youth apprenticeship arose in the first place because the schools have generally ignored the learning that may be gained in the work experience. For the most part, schools have not found ways to connect students' work experience with the school experience. And if a student leaves high school before graduating, to go to work, he or she is written off as a dropout, even though the student may be learning as much or more on the job than he or she did in school. I certainly do not want to encourage students to drop out of school! But I do believe schools could do a far better job of integrating students' work experience into their school experience.

One result of the lack of connection between school and work is that students emerge with the idea that there is a vast difference between "work learning" and "school learning." Studies of adult illiterates show this perception clearly. Many of these adults learn how to fix cars, do some plumbing, paint a house, or even own a business. They develop confidence in their abilities to learn to do these things, but they totally lack the same confidence in school learning. In fact, their attitudes toward formal schooling are often what keep them from participating in literacy programs. How much better to instill from an early age the idea that learning is learning, that all learning is connected, and that learning in one area can build on learning in another.

A RIGHT-SIDE-UP VIEW OF SCHOOLS THAT WORK TODAY

Much has been written in recent decades about the failure of American schools. But I would submit that our schools have *not* failed. For the past one hundred years, in fact, the public schools have been doing exactly what they were designed to do . . . to sort and label and separate the winners from the losers. The so-called academically successful winners in the education race went on to the university and became the leaders in our society. In the meantime, it was hoped that the rest of the students would pick up as much knowledge as possible and become contributing members in our society. The problem with this scheme is that it just doesn't fit today's reality. The successful schools of yesterday have been overtaken by the events of this new techno-information age.

Most of our school systems today operate more or less on an industrial-age assembly-line model. The educational assembly line moves along at a nine-month pace on a twelve-, fourteen-, or sixteen-year schedule. During that time, with wonderful occasional exceptions (particularly in elementary schools), students are taught in more or less the same way—a textbook-oriented, information-filled, cover-the-material approach. Students tend to be passive learners and not deeply involved in their subjects. There is little inquiry teaching and discovery learning. Problem-solving and critical-thinking skills are not usually taught directly, although it is hoped that students will somehow develop these competencies on their own.

Schools are expected to function as learning factories. The same methods and material are basically used for all students regardless of individual background or need. The unspoken message for teachers is: Just do your job and leave the systems thinking to your superiors—and don't worry about the defective products because someone at the end of the educational line will handle the problem cases with some kind of remedial education at the postsecondary level.[2]

What has been the result of this kind of assembly-line education? In essence, a system that educates one kind of student well and fails the rest of the students miserably. William Raspberry, syndicated columnist for the *Washington Post*, reports on research done by Ian Westbury of the University of Illinois:

> The top 20 percent of American students outscore the top 20 percent of Japanese students . . . American kids in the upper 50 percent of American classes score as well as or better than Japanese kids in the upper 50 percent of Japanese classes. . . . However Japanese kids in the lower half don't score all that far behind their upper-half peers. American kids in the lower half are far behind both the upper half of American classes and the lower half of Japanese classes. . . . The American bottom half, largely urban and rural poor, are in serious difficulty in spite of much of the reform now taking place.[3]

A RIGHT-SIDE-UP LOOK AT TEACHING THAT WORKS: A COMPARISON STUDY

One of the most interesting recent bits of research on improving American education has been done by James Stigler of the University of Chicago and Harold Stevenson of the University of Michigan. First and fifth graders from 120 classrooms in three different cities in three countries—Taipei in Taiwan, Sendai in Japan, and the Minneapolis area in the United States—were given a mathematics test that required computation and problem-solving skills. Only fifteen of the one hundred top-scoring first graders were American, and only one American student was among the top one hundred fifth graders.

Stigler and Stevenson also compared a representative sample of forty first-grade and forty fifth-grade classrooms in the metropolitan Chicago area to twenty-two classrooms in each of these grades in Beijing. In mathematics, they found no area in which the American students were competitive with Chinese students.

This dismal comparison of math performance between U.S. students and Chinese and Japanese students motivated Stigler and Stevenson to dig for the reasons behind it. These professors have written extensively about cultural differences and attitudes toward learning among children of these different cultures, but they became convinced that cultural differences alone cannot explain the performance differences they observed. So they decided to look at how math is actually taught in their sample of classrooms in China, Japan, and the United States. Their analysis and conclusions are instructive for us as we consider the characteristics of a right-side-up education.

Here is a boiled-down version of what they discovered about the way Japanese and Chinese classrooms worked.

Lessons Emphasize Problem Solving Rather Than Rote Learning

Rather than drilling students on memorized facts (with flash cards, multiplication tables, equations, and the like), the Japanese and Chinese teachers use many different kinds of representational materials and sample problems. They geared their lessons toward problem solving rather than rote learning.

Lessons Begin With a Problem and Solution Discovery

It is not uncommon for the Asian teacher to organize a full lesson around finding the solution to a single problem. Classroom lessons in China and Japan almost always begin with a practical problem. Mathematical computation skills are not ignored, but they are always presented in the context of problem solving.

Teachers Review the Material Thoroughly

The researchers found that fifth-grade teachers in China and Japan spend more time (eight times as much) reviewing and summarizing at the end of the class period than do teachers in the U.S.

Asian Teachers Handle Diversity by Developing a Variety of Real-Life Problems

Contrary to common belief, Asian classes are not homogenous. Teachers in China, Taiwan, and Japan must cope with individual differences among students just as teachers in the U.S. must. It is diversity in educational background, not in cultural background, that poses the biggest challenge for teachers in all four countries. Asian teachers seem to believe, however, that connecting knowing with doing is an effective way to meet the diversity challenge. They work hard at developing a variety of practical problems for the students to solve.

Asian Teachers Work from the Concrete to the Abstract, Not the Other Way Around

Asian teachers rely primarily upon the manipulation of concrete objects to teach math, believing that the effective use of hands-on examples will give students a better understanding of mathematics. The typical approach to a lesson in the United States sample schools was to first define terms and state rules for the lesson, then use practical examples to illustrate. Asian teachers tend to reverse this procedure by relating a real-world problem first.

Stigler and Stevenson give the following example of a Japanese teacher introducing third graders to the concept of fractions:

> The lesson began with the teacher posing the question of how many liters of juice (colored water) were contained in a large beaker. 'More than one liter,' answered one child. 'One and a half liters,' answered another. After several children had made guesses, the teacher suggested that they pour the juice into some one-liter beakers and see. Horizontal lines on each beaker divided it into thirds. The juice filled one beaker and part of a second. The teacher pointed out that the water came up to the first line on the second beaker—only one of the three parts was full. The procedure was repeated with a second set of beakers to illustrate the concept of one-half. After stating that there had been one and one-out-of-three liters of juice in the first big beaker and one and one-out-of-two liters in the second, the teacher wrote the fractions on the board. He continued the lesson by asking the children how to represent two parts out of three, two parts out of five, and so forth. Near the end of the period he mentioned the term 'fraction' for the first time and attached names to the numerator and the denominator. He ended the lesson by summarizing how fractions can be used to represent the parts of a whole.[4]

Asian elementary school classrooms are all usually equipped with many concrete objects for teachers to use in illustrating a lesson. Japanese classrooms feature a math set box full of colorful materials such as tiles, clocks, rulers, checkerboards, colored triangles, beads and other concrete objects. Teachers in China have fewer resources, so they improvise with plates, wax fruit, colored paper, and homemade objects. Many American teachers also improvise and develop homemade materials, but they still tend to begin lessons with abstract concepts and use the concrete objects later as illustrations.

Asian Teachers Communicate More

The Asian teachers appear to consult with each other about the development of class lessons much more than their American counterparts. In all three Pacific Rim countries studied, teachers spoke together daily about their lessons, particularly about developing questions to stimulate thought. The researchers report,

> One [Japanese elementary] teacher we interviewed told us of discussions she had with her fellow teachers on how to improve teaching practices. 'What do you talk about?' we wondered. 'A great deal of time,' she reported, 'is spent talking about questions we can pose to the class—which wordings work best to get students involved in thinking and discussing the material. One good question can keep a whole class going for a long time; a bad one produces little more than a simple answer.[5]

A major obstacle that prevents American teachers from communicating with each other on a regular basis is the simple problem of time. Preparing lessons that require student involvement and the discovery of knowledge is a time-consuming proposition. When teachers teach all day, every day throughout a school year, little time or energy is left for cooperative lesson planning.

One way Asian schools have solved the time problem is by having class sizes considerably larger than in most U.S. schools. This gives Asian teachers about the same student-teacher ratios within a school as U.S. teachers, but fewer actual teaching hours. For example, Japanese elementary schoolteachers are in charge of classes only about two-thirds of the time they are at schools.

Asian and U.S. teachers put in about the same amount of time working at the job of teaching, but the management of time is arranged quite differently. Asian teachers, for example, spend more time in the actual school building than American teachers. When they are at school, they have the time to meet with other teachers, work with children who need extra help, and develop lesson plans, but when they leave the school building they leave their work behind. Teachers in the United States may leave the school building earlier than Asian teachers, but they take the work home, working in isolation from their colleagues.

Another barrier to better communication between American teachers is the physical setup of the schools and the physical facilities provided to teachers. American teachers are by and large isolated from other teachers. They keep their teaching materials in their own classrooms or, in colleges, in their private offices. The only common space where they can meet together is usually a cramped room with a few chairs and a coffee machine. In the Asian schools studied, however, each teacher has a desk in a large room. It is in this room that teachers prepare lessons, compare notes, and engage in serious cooperative-learning discussions.

Asian Teachers Receive Training and Support

Graduates of Asian teacher-training institutions are considered to be first-year apprentices and can teach under the guidance of a master teacher. By Japanese law, beginning teachers must receive a minimum of twenty days inservice training. All teachers are required continually to improve their teaching techniques through interaction with other teachers. Teachers often meet together in study groups where one teacher teaches a lesson and the others evaluate it and suggest how the lesson can be improved.

Now contrast this system with American teacher training and inservice programs. Students emerge from most teacher training institutions in the United States with scant knowledge about how to design and teach effective contextual lessons. Most teachers in the United States lament that what they learned about teaching had to be learned on the job and in relative isolation.

What Can We Learn from China, Taiwan, and Japan?

This lengthy review of comparative educational systems has not been presented for the purposes of running down American schools and teachers. And I certainly do not want to imply that the Japanese and Chinese education systems are perfect and should be imported to this country. However, I believe we can glean from these other cultures some ideas about a right-side-up education that may help us improve our own American-style system of education.

Table 1
What Does a Right-Side-Up Classroom Look Like?

The Upside-Down Classroom (Conventional Classroom)	The Right-Side-Up Classroom (LogoLearning Classroom)
Knowledge and the presentation of knowledge are the only important parts of the teaching-learning process.	Helping students understand the application of knowledge is as important as dispensing knowledge.
Thinking is usually done in theoretical and academic terms.	Thinking involves making the connection between knowing and doing with "real-life" problem-solving issues.
Students routinely work and study alone.	Students routinely work with teachers and peers in cooperative learning.
Lessons usually begin with theory or learning exercises that emphasize memorization.	Lessons usually begin with examples or problems from real-world experiences and then move out to interactively combine content with context.

Academic and vocational education are approached as though in isolation.	Academic and vocational education concepts are integrated wherever possible.
Teachers tend to plan lessons and teach in isolation from colleagues.	Teacher colleagues plan lessons together and team teach wherever possible.
Time is the constant and competence is the variable.	Student mastery is the constant and time is the variable.

THE FIVE BASIC PRINCIPLES OF THE RIGHT-SIDE-UP EDUCATION

For this past century, American educational institutions have kept the teaching-learning process and curriculum structure as the constants and allowed the results to vary. (They have varied greatly.) LogoLearning holds that we must turn that system right-side-up by making teaching and curriculum the variables and results the constant. We must adjust our teaching methods and curricula as necessary to produce consistent, high-performance outcomes for all students. This represents a real break-the-mold education.

FIVE BASIC PRINCIPLES

Right-Side-Up Principle #1:
Purpose Directs the Organization

Right-Side-Up Principle #2:
Real-Life Problems Take Precedence Over Subject-Matter Isolation

Right-Side-Up Principle #3:
Students Gain Understanding Through Problem Solving

Right-Side-Up Principle #4:
Academic and Vocational Concerns Are Integrated Whenever Possible into an Applied-Learning Process

Right-Side-Up Principle #5:
Competence Is the Constant; Time the Variable

What are the chief characteristics of the right-side-up education? We have explored them throughout this book, but I want to summarize them here by listing five basic principles:

Right-Side-Up Principle #1: Purpose Directs the Organization

The outcomes of an educational endeavor are important. But as Edwards Deming said so many times, concentrating primarily upon outcomes with little attention to purpose is like endeavoring to drive a car by looking only in the rear-view mirror. Outcome statements must flow out of purpose, and there must be a high resolve to maintain a constancy of purpose throughout the entire organization.

Education can learn from the mistakes made by American business, particularly large corporations. They have evidenced a nearsightedness by giving priority attention to short-term goals and quick profit and by viewing staff training as an expense rather than an investment. Corporate purposes or mission statements are usually developed by corporate directors and officers with little involvement by the frontline workers, and consequently these workers show little commitment to company goals.

The same can be said for many schools and colleges. Too many educational organizations lack a constancy of purpose and as a consequence they often latch onto an array of contradicting practices and outcome statements. Mission statements and goals are often developed by politicians, boards of directors, and administrators, which usually motivates little commitment from the teachers and other staff. In addition, as we have seen, the goals are usually so broad as to be meaningless, or they are stated only as derived outcomes unconnected to purpose.

Quite often in our educational organizations we have let our traditional assumptions about how education is supposed to proceed get in the way of a clear vision of what education is supposed to accomplish. In other words, people teach the way they have been taught, organize schools the way they have always been organized, and don't stop to question the "why" of these methods and structures and philosophies. For instance, in many areas the domination of subject-matter disciplines—math for math's sake, science for science's sake, English for English's sake, history for history's sake—has all but eliminated discussion of overall educational purpose. In assuming that "students have to learn math, students need English, students need history," and so forth, we don't stop to think, "What are we trying to accomplish in this teaching endeavor?" "How will this help a student deal with real life issues?"

If we are serious about turning education right side up, some changes are required. We must examine our assumptions about what education is supposed to accomplish and put some serious thought into considering "why." An overarching sense of purpose, built around the life role human commonalities, with related anticipated outcomes must direct the scope and sequence of the curriculum, which in turn must direct the teaching process and motivate learning for all but the most specialized programs and institutions.

Right-Side-Up Principle #2: Real-Life Problems Take Precedence Over Subject-Matter Isolation

LogoLearning takes exception to the usual isolation of the teaching-learning process from real-world situations. All of us live with the impact of political organizations, government agencies, financial institutions, business and industry, cultural and religious groups, labor unions, and particularly the information media of television, radio, newspapers, and other publications. Yet, in too many instances the school curriculum and teaching-learning process seem to bear little relationship to this real-world context in which students live now and in which they will spend their future lives.

A right-side-up education turns that situation around by directly and specifically relating school study to real-life problems and real-life learning situations.

Lauren Resnick of the Learning Research Development Center at the University of Pittsburgh has developed a comparative analysis of how individuals learn in contemporary schooling and how they learn in real-life situations. Her comparison can be instructive to any educator interested in bringing school and work closer together.[6]

Table 2
School Learning and Life Learning

SCHOOL LEARNING	REAL LIFE LEARNING
• abstract learning (content emphasis)	• applied learning (context emphasis)
• symbol manipulation (memorizing)	• problem solving (reasoning)
• individual learning (working alone)	• cooperative learning (teamwork)
• general learning (from the general to specific)	• concrete learning (from the specific to general)

Audrey Cohen, president and founder of Audrey Cohen College in New York City and leader of an education reform project funded by the New American Schools Development Corporation, calls the move toward real-life involvement "Constructive Action." She advocates that, during each stage of learning, students carry out some individual or group activity that furthers the learning process and connects the academic material directly to real-world problems. Here is a specific example of an age-appropriate Constructive Action involving student examination of their own diet and physical hygeine:

Suppose, for example, that the purpose for a learning stage for 9-year-olds is to work for better health. Such a purpose is particularly appropriate at this age because it pinpoints developmental needs of children at the same time that it involves them in Constructive Action. Children at this age are capable of taking responsibility for their own diet and physical hygiene. It is important that they do so because they are frequently surrounded by negative health messages (fast-food restaurants, cigarette smoking, alcoholism, and so on). Indeed, it is a sad commentary on our system of education that, while it provides children with intellectual knowledge, it so rarely enables them to take charge of their lives in important practical ways.[7]

Lessons gain authenticity (and are better retained by students) when the lesson themes and classroom activities clearly connect to issues and experiences outside the classroom. This can be done in a number of ways ranging from simple examples, to field trips, to interdisciplinary projects. To be effective, however, the experiences and examples must be meaningful to the student.

Textbooks from other countries, on the whole, tend to provide better examples of connections to real-world situations. However, even other countries have problems with students making the connection with real-world situations. In 1993, Frank Horvath, Director of Student Evaluation in Alberta, Canada, made these comments to a newspaper on achievement results in one province of his country:

> Horvath said social studies students had a good understanding of basic concepts, but had difficulty applying their knowledge. They slipped up in areas like understanding levels of government, and knowledge about Pacific Rim countries—studying China is one Grade 6 level topic.
>
> In science, students did well recalling basic concepts, "as long as they are within familiar context . . . but they have a lot of difficulty applying what they learn to real life situations, or situations they haven't encountered before," said Horvath.
>
> "When it comes to problem-solving, they have a tendency to jump to conclusions, to pay insufficient attention to inconsistencies or missing information, and they fail to look for alternative solutions or see other possibilities, which is fundamental to science."[8]

The responsibility to help students see connections falls heavily upon the teacher. Much credit, therefore, must be given to the leadership provided by the American Association for the Advancement of Science, the National Science

Teachers Association, the National Council of Teachers of Mathematics, and the National Council of Teachers of English (along with other national groups) for their leadership efforts in developing teaching-learning materials and processes aimed at bringing education and real-life issues closer together.

As it turns out, these national groups have also concluded that traditional subject-matter disciplines are not the best ways to organize for teaching about reality. They do not integrate easily with one another, nor do they regularly disclose the nature of real-world activity. Too often subject-matter disciplines have become the ends rather than a means to an end, the purpose of teaching rather than an organizational tool.

This upside-down situation must be turned right side up. We urgently need students at all levels of education who can put their learning into real-life perspective and then put their learning to work. For this to happen, I urge a more thematic and connected approach to the teaching-learning process.

Right-Side-Up Principle #3: Students Gain Understanding Through Problem Solving

Problem-based learning is a great way to turn the teaching-learning process right side up. With this approach to teaching, students are introduced to a problem *before* the knowledge-acquisition instruction begins. In lieu of covering a prescribed textbook lesson, teachers help students grapple with a problem and then use knowledge (both what they know and what they can find out) to develop solutions.

In a problem-based scenario, students assume the roles of workers, home-makers, historians, politicians, or other people attempting to solve real-life problems. They realize very quickly that there are several sides to a problem and that bias can enter every point of view. They learn the value of teamwork in solving the problems, and they quickly realize that they must call on information from many different subject areas in order to solve a given problem.

Teachers take on a new role as well in a problem-based situation. They must act like a student, thinking aloud with students, guiding and directing them. Teachers in such a situation quickly learn the art of Socratic questioning: What do we need to know more about? Can there be more than one solution to this problem? What lessons can we learn?

At least three types of problem-based learning have been identified: student-centered learning, problem-stimulated learning, and post-hole problems.

Student-centered learning is most often used in high school or college settings. The instructor presents a problem with the goal of fostering the knowledge and skills required by a given lesson. However, the instructor does not specify in advance the content to be mastered or the resources to be utilized. The students work in teams to identify the learning issues they want to explore and the resources on which they must draw. The teacher serves as a resource to the teams, guides the action, and keeps the teams on track.

Problem-stimulated learning is most often used in the earlier grades, but it can also appear throughout the education continuum. This approach is teacher driven; the teacher provides a list of objectives outlining material and skills students are expected to master, a list of suggested references, and a set of predeveloped discussion questions. Students then work in teams with these materials, and each student is assigned a particular role on the team (leader, recorder, or team member). Here, too, in addition to preparing the objectives and materials, the teacher serves as a resource and a guide.

Post-hole problems are an increasingly popular way of bringing problem-based learning into classrooms at all levels. "Post holes" are brief problems that can be used at the beginning of a lesson to motivate interest or can be brought in from time to time in situations where teachers do not want to gear all teaching to problem solving. Social studies teachers and science teachers at DeWitt Clinton High School in the Bronx, New York, coined the term *post holes* and have created a whole series of these "quickie" problems to be utilized in their history, government, and science classes. They see these mini-problems as tools both for helping students develop problem-solving skills and for helping them understand content within the context of application.[9]

Right-Side-Up Principle #4: Academic and Vocational Concerns Are Integrated Whenever Possible into an Applied-Learning Process

For many years, educators have relegated academic education and vocational education to separate worlds. This separation was exemplified by saying there are people who work with their heads, and there are people who work with their hands—and it was assumed that the two would never meet. Students in the academic disciplines, especially the college prep programs, were assumed not to need any specific preparation for the world of work. And "voc ed" students were expected to train for specific jobs; they were assumed to have little need for competency in "academic" fields.

Public opinion has followed that line of thinking, along with the corollary assumption that vocational education is essentially inferior education. But such attitudes and assumptions, which were never based entirely on truth, are completely out of step with the realities of today's workplace. A highly competitive job market makes preparation for the human commonality of work a necessity for all students, not just "voc ed" students. At the same time, the drying up of high-pay, low-skill jobs and the volatility of the job market demand that *all* students achieve greater academic competencies and that many more students move on to some form of postsecondary education. (It is estimated that the large majority of jobs in the next decade will require more than a high school education but less than a four-year baccalaureate degree.)

What all this means is that the schism between academic education and vocational education must be healed. *All* students require better academic competencies along with better preparation for the life role of work, and the majority of students desperately require academic subjects to be taught the way they learn best—in an application-based, contextual environment.

Fortunately, a national movement has been developing since the mid-1980s that urges the integration of academic and vocational education. As I write, the applied-learning movement has grown into a full-fledged educational reform movement that promises to transform the way America does education.

In 1987, the Southern Regional Education Board (SREB) formed a Vocational Education Consortium. This highly successful program, which includes nineteen states with over one hundred sites, was formed specifically for the purpose of integrating academic and vocational education through the development of applied-learning techniques. In 1992, under the leadership of Gene Bottoms, the SREB developed a publication entitled *Making High Schools Work,* which distilled the experience of a half-dozen years into a coherent statement of what applied learning is all about (see table 3).

Table 3
Elements of Applied Learning[10]

1.CONTENT KNOWLEDGE

Academic Knowledge	Specific concepts, facts, and procedures drawn from college preparatory language arts, mathematics, and science curricula
Learning and Problem-Solving	How to learn new concepts, facts, and procedures. For example, using reading and writing techniques to learn subject matter. Students are introduced to strategies used by teachers and experts in academic and vocational fields to solve problems and apply academic contents to new situations.
Technical Knowledge and Skills	Technical subject matter and specific problems, procedures, and tasks for broad occupational fields of study.

2. EFFECTIVE METHODS

Build on Experiences and Potential Uses	Introduce new concepts, facts, and procedures by relating them to students' past knowledge and experiences. Relate the concepts, facts, and procedures to

	specific situations students are likely to encounter in the future.
Make Connections	Encourage students to verbalize and share connections between what they learn in academic and vocational classes.
Focus on the Whole Task to Be Learned	Help students visualize the whole task they are being asked to learn before they break it into smaller parts.
Use New Knowledge	Allow students to use new knowledge in the context of working through a real problem.
Reinforce Academic Knowledge	Encourage students to verbalize academic competencies they will need to solve a job-related problem or perform a task.
Cooperative Learning	Students work together to accomplish their goals in academic and vocational classes and across classes.
Joint Learning Projects	Academic and vocational teachers work together to help students learn how to use academic knowledge and competencies to accomplish a work-oriented task or product. In the spirit of traditional apprenticeships, this approach provides students with guidance and support for individual and group projects.

3. SCHOOL CLIMATE AND ORGANIZATION

Interdisciplinary Staff Strategies	The school organization promotes inter-disciplinary teams of academic and vocational teachers working together to improve academic learning.
Student Schedules and Assignments	The school schedule and student assignments allow teachers to share a group of students.

Leadership	Schools encourage and reward collaboration among academic and vocational teachers, including arranging time in the schedule for them to meet and plan together.

Contextual learning principles have been successfully incorporated into curriculum development by organizations such as the Center for Occupational Research and Development (CORD) in Waco, Texas and the Agency for Instructional Technology (AIT) in Bloomington, Indiana. In the mid-1980s, under the leadership of Dan Hull, president of CORD, these two organizations pulled together resources from more than forty states to begin a multimillion-dollar contextual learning curriculum development effort. Courses that have been developed as a part of this effort include the following:

- *Principles of Technology* is an applied physics course, a two-year curriculum covering fourteen units in physics and mathematics. Lab work and real-world applications keep the focus on actual problems encountered in the workforce and in everyday experience.

- *Applied Mathematics, a Contextual Approach to Integrated Mathematics (formerly referred to as Applied Math)* combines the content of traditional algebra, geometry, trigonometry, and statistics taught in a real-world context and features the use of calculators and computers to solve problems.

- *Applications in Biology/Chemistry, a Contextual Approach to Laboratory Science (formerly Applied Biology/Chemistry or ABC)* focuses study on water, air, gases, plant growth and reproduction, nutrition, disease and wellness. A wealth of laboratory activities helps students understand how similar tests and experiments are conducted in the work settings.

- *Applied Communication* are applied English courses aimed at improving student competencies in writing, speaking, reading, group interaction, giving and taking instructions, and conflict resolution especially as these skills apply in job situations. These courses have been developed on a module basis so they can be used as units in regular English classes or as stand-alone courses.[11]

Other organizations have also been active in developing applied-learning courses:

- *Applied Economics* is an excellent one-semester secondary school-level economics course developed by the Junior Achievement organization, which also furnishes business consultants to speak in the classrooms.

- *Materials Science Technology* is a problem-solving course developed by the Battelle Pacific Northwest Laboratories and the Northwest Regional Educational Laboratory.
- *Chemistry in the Community* (ChemCom) is a hands-on applied chemistry course developed by the American Chemical Society. It covers the conventional concepts of chemistry courses with a particular emphasis on critical thinking and problem solving.
- *School Mathematics Project* was developed at the University of Chicago as a mathematics curriculum for grades seven through twelve. The courses that make up the project emphasize how to apply math to real-world situations.

In addition to the formal development of applied-learning courses, many local schools and school districts are developing contextual-learning teams to develop or modify local courses. These applied-learning task forces have been highly successful in providing desired teaching-learning experiences. Some of their projects are described in chapter 6 of this book.

The Tech Prep/Associate Degree curriculum plan has been perhaps the most talked-about aspect of the contextual-learning movement. Often referred to simply as tech prep, this innovative approach to education was first outlined in my 1985 book, *The Neglected Majority*.[12] That publication was followed by a nationwide discussion on developing the program and by the development of pilot programs across the country. Now almost ten years old, the Tech Prep/Associate Degree program has developed into a mature educational reform movement, and the United States Congress is now providing funds to implement the program across the country.

Essentially, the Tech Prep/Associate Degree program is a structured, articulated four-year curriculum involving the last two years of high school and the freshman and sophomore years in a community college or technical school. Students are taught by high school teachers during their first two years of the tech prep program, but have access to community or technical college personnel and facilities where appropriate. The third and fourth years of the program are taught at the community college by college faculty and culminate in the earning of an associate degree or a certificate of mastery in a given profession. At that point students are ready for employment in any number of careers or paraprofessional jobs ranging from engineering technology to law enforcement to nursing to bookkeeping to aeronautics to auto technology.

The Tech Prep/Associate Degree features the following characteristics:

- It is a partnership program involving secondary and postsecondary (technical school or community college) personnel, academic and vocational teachers, employers and educators all working together.

- It is a program that provides students with a solid academic base of science, math, communications, and technical education courses, all taught in an applied, contextual manner.
- It is a program with scope and sequence structure, academic substance, and a clear focus for the student, ending with an associate degree or certificate of competency in a career area.
- It is a program of excellence that provides the student with high-level employment skills, meets the high standards for the associate degree, and may also, in some cases, be applied toward the requirements of a baccalaureate degree.
- It is a step beyond the usual high school and college articulation agreements, involving substantive curricular change and a high degree of coordination between high school and college. Secondary and college faculty work together as colleagues to develop the curriculum and guide students through it.
- It is a program designed particularly for that "neglected majority" of students who are not likely to earn a four-year college baccalaureate degree, although recent experiences indicate that all students can profit from its contextual-learning approach to education.

Tech Prep/Associate Degree programs can now be found in every state of the union (the implementation process varies from state to state). Those schools that have had extensive experience in implementing them claim significant progress, high school dropout rates are declining, academic-achievement test scores are going up, many more high school students are going on to postsecondary education. Perhaps most important, students are enjoying learning, and teachers testify to a renewed sense of joy in their work. Chapter 6 describes a few outstanding examples of schools and colleges where Tech Prep/Associate Degree programs are making a difference.

Right-Side-Up Principle #5: Competence Is the Constant; Time the Variable

Here is one of the most perplexing conundrums in all of education: It is widely recognized by teachers (and even students) that students learn at different rates of speed. Yet, with rare exceptions, we still force students to learn whatever they can during a given time period, whether that be a week, a quarter, a semester, or a school year. In most of our educational systems, time is the constant and competence is the variable. In a right-side-up educational system, the reverse should be true.

What would you think of a physician who told you, "I am giving you one week (or ten weeks) to get well, and if you are not well by then I shall fail you and consider you a bad patient!"?

Or let's bring the illustration closer to the subject at hand. What would you think of the teacher who told students, "You have nine weeks to learn this material, and if you don't learn it during that time period you will be given a failing grade?" Teachers may not say it, but that's exactly what our typical time structure in education tells students.

If educators really believe that students naturally learn at different rates, then we must restructure our school days and school year and our testing-grading practices accordingly. Can it be that many students now labeled as average simply learn at a different rate of speed? Which is more important, to test students on what they should know and give them an opportunity to learn what they have missed, or to give a final test and final grade based upon what they have managed to learn during an arbitrary nine-week grading period?

In some schools and colleges, and in many university graduate programs, students receive either an A or B or C grade or an Incomplete, which remains on the student record until such time as the student can learn the material and complete course requirements. Typically, under current practices, the Incomplete will turn to an F after a period of one or two semesters. Surely such a system, which allows for a certain flexibility in completing course requirements, would apply in many other educational situations. (Actually, I question why an Incomplete couldn't remain on a student record forever or until made up. What's the point of turning it into a failing grade?)

I have already pointed out that our schools and colleges, by and large, still operate on the industrial-age factory model. That applies to their time schedules as well. Education is conducted on the assembly-line model of Carnegie Units or credit hours and quarters or semesters. Is it time to reconsider? Perhaps the Carnegie Unit, historically expressed in terms of time (hours) could be changed to represent some unit of competence instead.

Perhaps it's time to revisit the work of Benjamin Bloom, of University of Chicago fame, whose concept of "mastery learning" was first spelled out in the 1956 *Taxonomy of Educational Objectives*.[13] In Bloom's model, students are given as much time as required to learn each lesson or learning task, and results are assessed in terms of either mastery or nonmastery. The teacher works with each student on the way to self-timed mastery, diagnosing any problems and providing special helps such as self-paced technology, tutors, student "coaches" (more advanced students who help others), rereading, and restudying.

Another important voice for mastery learning is that of John Carroll, Director of the Psychometrics Laboratory at the University of North Carolina, who developed his own model of mastery learning in 1963.[14] Carroll insists that one of the worst things we do in education is to not allow a student adequate time to master one lesson before moving to the next lesson. Carroll's list of five elements or factors in learning—three depending on the student and two depending on the teacher—sheds fascinating light on the essentials of the learning process and helps put the time factor into perspective:

- **Student-Dependent Factors**
    1. Aptitude (the amount of time the student needs to master a learning task)
    2. Ability to understand instruction (primarily on verbal and written)
    3. Perseverance (the amount of time the learner is willing to spend on a task)

- **Teacher-Dependent Factors**
    1. Quality of instruction (the degree to which a lesson is made real and understandable for the student)
    2. Time allowed for learning (the quantity of time allowed for learning)

Even though Bloom and Carroll are considered to be heavily influenced by behaviorist theories, we can learn much from them when it comes to righting the upside-down approach to time in most of our educational institutions.

A RIGHT-SIDE-UP EDUCATION MEANS THE BEST OF BOTH WORLDS

The whole idea of a right-side-up education—the LogoLearning education—is that if you put first things first, the second things (and the third, and the fourth) will fall into their place. LogoLearning gives unabashed first priority to constancy of purpose in education, integration of content with context, utilizing problem-based teaching, integrating wherever possible academic and vocational education, and making competence the constant and time the variable.

That doesn't mean the second things will be abandoned. Insisting that dates and numbers and body parts be learned within the context of their real-world application doesn't mean those dates and numbers and body parts won't be learned. More likely, teaching those facts in context increases the probability that they will actually be understood and retained for use in new problem-solving situations.

LogoLearning is not an either-or education. Instead, it is an integrated approach that provides a bridge between:

- purpose *and* outcome
- head *and* hand
- academic *and* vocational
- knowing *and* doing
- theory *and* practice
- time *and* competence
- education *and* training

For all students in our schools and colleges, and especially for those who over the years have been sorted and labeled instead of provided with the meaningful education they deserve, LogoLearning provides an education that connects. It's an education that provides meaning for the student and engages the student in thought. It is truly a right-side-up approach to education.

---

1 People for the American Way, *Democracy's Next Generation* (Washington, D.C., 1989).

2 Many years ago Harold Benjamin, Emeritus Professor of Education at the George Peabody College for Teachers in Nashville (now Peabody University) wrote a humorous little book entitled *The Saber-Tooth Curriculum* (New York: McGraw-Hill, 1939). In it he reported upon mythical research that claimed to unveil three fundamental skills taught to paleolithic children. These were "fish grabbing with the bare hands," "horse clubbing," and "saber-tooth tiger scaring with fire." When a glacier caused tigers, horses, and fish to disappear, schools nevertheless went on teaching these "eternal verities." Benjamin's wry little story beautifully targets our contemporary reluctance to abandon the industrial-age assembly-line model of education.

3 William Raspberry, "Best U.S. Students Test Well Against Other Nations," *Washington Post*, 16 October 1993.

4 James W. Stigler and Harold W. Stevenson, "How Asian Teachers Polish Each Lesson to Perfection," *American Federation of Teachers Journal*, Spring 1991, 20.

5 Stigler and Stevenson, "How Asian Teachers Polish," 43.

6 Lauren Resnick, "Learning In School and Out," *Educational Researcher*, December 1987, 13–20.

7 Audrey Cohen, "A New Educational Paradigm," *Phi Delta Kappan*, June 1993, 793.

8 Frank Horvath, "Many Kids Fall Below Standard," *Calgary Herald*, 11 November 1993.

9 William Stepien and Shelagh Gallagher, "Problem-Based Learning: As Authentic As It Gets," *Educational Leadership*, April 1993, 28.

10 Gene Bottoms, Alice Presson, and Mary Johnson, *Making High Schools Work: Through Integration of Academic and Vocational Education* (Atlana: Southern Regional Education Board, 1992), 53–54.

11 For more information on these contextual-learning courses and the whole subject of contextual learning, see Dan Hull, *Opening Minds, Opening Doors: The Rebirth of American Education* (Waco: CORD, 1993) or contact the Center for Occupational Research and Development (CORD), P.O. Box 21689, Waco, TX 76702, or telephone 1-800-972-2766.

12 Dale Parnell, *The Neglected Majority* (Washington, D.C.: Community College Press, 1985). The Community College Press can be contacted at One Dupont Circle, Washington, D.C. 20036.

13 Benjamin S. Bloom, ed., *Taxonomy of Educational Objectives Handbook: Cognitive Domain* (New York: McKay, 1956). See also *All Our Children Learning* (New York: McGraw-Hill, 1981).

14 Sylvia Farnham-Diggory, *Cognitive Processes in Education* (New York: Harper-Collins, 1992). This book is highly recommended for those wishing to study the development of cognitive science and the cognitive apprenticeship model.

15 For more information about Tech Prep/Association Degree see Dan Hull and Dale Parnell, eds., *Tech Prep Associate Degree: A Win/Win Experience.* (Waco: Center for Occupational Research and Development, 1991).

CHAPTER 6

Education That Works

Exemplary Practices in LogoLearning

We now know a lot more about learning, and we know that a lot of people with very high intelligence levels learn better in practical settings. And we also know that practical skills now require higher-order thinking. So the old dividing line between vocational and academic [education] is fast becoming blurred and will become more and more meaningless as time goes on.

–President Bill Clinton

*L*ogoLearning lives! Its principles have always undergirded the most effective teaching and its ideas have long been supported by some of the great names in twentieth-century education. But now the momentum is gathering. Teachers, administrators, and educational leaders across the nation are beginning to catch the LogoLearning vision and to turn education in this country right side up.

That growing momentum is what I want to chronicle in this chapter. Here you have a kind of LogoLearning sampler, and it is only a sampler, a collection of success stories from elementary schools, middle schools, secondary schools, and postsecondary institutions across the country.

But I must begin with an apology. In a country as large as the United States, with its hugely diverse and widely decentralized education system, it is next to impossible to paint an adequate or complete picture of LogoLearning at work. Unfortunately, most of the teachers practicing what we have been preaching about LogoLearning do not have the time to publish, and modesty prevents many from talking about what works for them. So to all those whose efforts have not yet come to my attention . . . my hat is off to you. I wish you many more years of meaningful teaching as you continue to explore the power and possibilities of LogoLearning at work.

LogoLearning at Work
in Elementary and Middle Schools

A Math Lesson for Lunch[1]

Mary Lindquist, president of the National Council of Teachers of Mathematics, tells of a first-grade classroom in Wisconsin. As the teacher collected lunch money from her twenty students, she discovered that eight students had brought their lunches that day. This was a good real-life opportunity for a math lesson, so she posed the question: "How many of you did not bring your lunches today?"

In a typical classroom, students would have been required to write out 20 – 8 on their papers. They would have focused upon memory rather than problem solving. But in this classroom, the students approached the problem in a variety of ways. Some students began to count on their fingers, some got out toy figures, and some used blocks. As could be expected, there were several answers to the lunch-count problem, and each child wanted to explain his or her answer before the teacher coached them through the problem.

Teachers like the one in that first-grade class recognize that students must use and see meaning in their math rather than just relying upon rote memorization. Getting the right answer is important, but understanding the process behind getting that answer is even more important.

When Ice Cream Goes KAPOW[2]

Sixth graders in Lowell Elementary School in Teaneck, New Jersey, have invented their own new flavors of Häagen-Dazs® ice cream. In the process, these students have traced the launch of a new product from start to finish, identifying the jobs involved and discussing such sophisticated subjects as quality control, nutrition, and marketing. Even though the company has no intention of marketing their exotic flavors, this problem-solving process results in an excellent applied-economics lesson.

The Grand Metropolitan Company, a British-owned food conglomerate, initially committed two million dollars to launch this elementary school program on a national basis. It is called KAPOW—Kids and the Power of Work. Volunteers from component Grand Met companies such as Pillsbury, Häagen-Dazs®, and Burger King lead a class once a month in nearby elementary schools. The goal is to establish a national program involving hundreds of interested businesses using the KAPOW curriculum in cooperation with local schools.

KAPOW volunteers include workers with many different roles in the companies—secretaries, research scientists, chief executive officers, mail clerks. One forklift operator explained to a class that although he liked his work, he was blocked from doing another job at higher pay because he did not yet have the required math competencies. Needless to say, the students got the message about learning their math lessons!

A Brand-New Way of Doing Things

Ardenwald and Seth Lewelling Elementary Schools in Milwaukie, Oregon,[3] have kicked off an innovative new concept in their multiage classrooms. As plans were being made for this new departure, the faculty at these two schools decided they needed a new teaching methodology to match their new multiage classroom structure. They began to develop contextually based teaching units that integrate several subject-matter disciplines into one lively lesson.

The faculty and staff at Ardenwald and Lewelling are so excited about this new direction for their schools that they have committed themselves to developing a whole new contextual-learning curriculum. Parents have been asked to involve themselves in contextual-learning experiences with their children. Representatives from local business are visible in the classrooms, providing real-life examples to bolster what the students are learning. Although it is too early in the development of this program to assess the quality of the program, early evaluations indicate much teacher excitement and optimism about the long-range increases in student learning.

If You Want to Learn, Teach![4]

Fifth- and sixth-grade teachers at T. K. Gorman Middle School and several other schools in Tyler, Texas look forward to the days when their economics teachers come to school. That is because their teachers are students from a local community college. Sophomore accounting students from Tyler Junior College (TJC) commit about twenty hours of personal time to study, prepare, and deliver four hands-on applied-economics lessons called Business Basics to classes of fifth and sixth graders. The college limits participation to sophomore accounting students because these students have had the most exposure to business courses. In addition, many of these students have jobs that help them in explaining the subject to younger students.

The TJC students are amazed at the speed with which middle school students listen to, grasp, and apply the business concepts they teach. And community college students are finding out that if you want to really learn something, you need to teach it.

Since Business Basics was introduced to Tyler schools in the fall of 1988, it has involved 965 students in 128 classes, with students from Tyler Junior College leading most of the classes. "I just love it" says Susan Rhodes, a fifth-grade teacher. "Tell me when you want me to stop raving about it. . . . I think it is as good for the students at Tyler Junior College as it is for my students, because they [the college students] don't realize just how sophisticated these fifth-graders are. They find out these kids are pretty wise to the ways of business."

Business Basics is sponsored by Junior Achievement (JA), a private nonprofit organization. JA is the oldest and most experienced business/education partnership in the nation. Founded in 1919, this organization now reaches more than 1.5 million students each year and is supported by twenty-four thousand companies.

Junior Achievement offers other applied economics programs to schools at no cost to the schools. In addition to the middle-school Business Basics program, there is an elementary-school program that focuses upon the basic concepts of goods and services and applied-economics issues. Project Business, a general business program for eighth and ninth graders, covers seven economics topics presented by a volunteer from the business world. For high-school students, JA offers Applied Economics as a one-semester course that helps students start their own small companies under the guidance of business personnel.

Getting into the Debt[5]

With the leadership of math teachers, students at Western View Middle School in Corvallis, Oregon, are participating in thematic projects that are part of the Oregon education and reform program. In one such project, students are studying the national debt. The students are trying to understand and solve a real-life problem that involves several different disciplines and calls for a host of interrelated facts and skills. The lessons require students to use facts and skills from math, English, social studies, and other areas of study. They must use computers, write out reports, find information in the library, and work as part of a team. As a test, the students give oral presentations. Then they evaluate themselves and they are also evaluated by their peers and by math teacher Mike Strowbridge.

Strowbridge indicates that the primary objective of this thematic lesson is to try and get students to use graphics and spreadsheets in a real-life context. Students use the computer to print out a pie chart detailing major government expenditures. He also notes that students really learn when they must present the lesson to someone else. However, he admits that directing such a project is much harder than just giving an assignment out of a textbook. The projects are time consuming for both teacher and students because so many different bits of knowledge and skills are involved.

In speaking of the project, student Mac Coakley says, "Math teachers always told me I would need this stuff someday when you know you're never going to use it again." Now, immersed in a real-life study of the national debt, Coakley and his classmates are beginning to see the connections between math and a real-world problem. "It is more interesting. . . . I'm dealing with stuff in the world today. You don't have to say you're never going to use this stuff."

But delving into the real world of economics has its down side as well—students come to realize just how serious the real-world national debt really is. Mac Coakley summarizes the project by saying: "It's depressing. I knew the debt was going up fast, but I never realized how fast. We computed the debt on the computer and it was so fast, you couldn't see it."

Doing Something About the Weather (and Other Simulating Topics)

Clear Choice Educational Products Company in Helm, Georgia[6] has developed a Weather Satellite Program that allows middle-school students to simulate a meteorologist's satellite imaging system. This interactive compact-disk simulation contains actual images from a satellite weather link-up, including an image of 1992's Hurricane Andrew. Students can manipulate the images and get information about temperatures, precipitation, and the like from graphs and color enhancements. Step-by-step instructions take the students through a complete course on satellite weather interpretation, involving them in problem solving, geography, math, vocabulary, science, and technology skills.

The Weather Satellite Program is only one of many new simulation lessons now being developed by commercial firms. The development of the optical video disk promises to offer educators a literal shelf-full of affordable interactive lessons that simulate real-life situations.[7]

Many businesses and government organizations have already seen the enormous educational potential of simulation programs. The armed services, for example, have moved with great speed to install such programs and use them in training programs. Airline pilots now receive most of their training via simulator. Simulation can duplicate exactly the control-feel dynamics of the airplane during take off, cruise, bad weather, wind shear, icy runways, landings, and brake and tire failures.

Foreign languages have proven to be a fertile field for simulator technology. The Air Force Academy has developed one such instructional program that utilizes self-paced interactive video disk instruction. A typical lesson will simulate being in a French restaurant and ordering from the menu in French. If the student needs help, he or she can call up a glossary showing the English translation of each word.

LogoLearning at Work in High Schools

Math with a Mission[8]

Donna Gaarder of Mission High School in San Francisco, California, has enjoyed considerable success using a nontraditional approach to teaching algebra, geometry, and trigonometry. Her method integrates all three sub-jects into a series of problems that the students are required to investigate. Group work is stressed, along with understanding of how solutions are reached. Front-of-the-classroom lectures and workbook exercises have been nearly eliminated in favor of student teams who work together to write papers and make oral presentations. Students are not grouped by ability, and all are expected to succeed.

Gaarder's innovative curriculum, known as the Interactive Mathematics Project, consists of a series of six-week units, each organized around a specific theme or problem. The lessons are designed to push students to think rather than simply plug information into memorized formulas. For example, Donna Gaarder asks her students why bees make hexagons instead of circles to build honeycombs. "It wouldn't be stable" says one student. Another student volunteers, "A hexagon has more space. You can store more honey that way." Working together, students grow toward understanding the characteristics of various geometric shapes.

Mission principal Patricia Aramendia is highly enthused about Gaarder's innovative approach to math. She testifies that Gaarder's applied-learning approach has transformed unmotivated, sleepy, and daydreaming students into active and lively learners who learn for meaning and understand what they are learning.

A Big Liftoff for the Central Project[9]

At McCullough High School in Conroe, Texas students, teachers, admin-istration and the community have come together to create a more meaningful learning experience for the students by means of an interdisciplinary exercise called the Central Project. They have found it to be a practical, effective, and inexpensive model for meaningful, reality-based education. In practice, it incorporates many of the theories and accomplishes many of the goals established by LogoLearning.

The Central Project began in 1987 with the Student Space Simulations (SSS). This was when the second-year architecture students took a different approach from typical residential and commercial buildings and worked to research, design, and build a habitat that would sustain four people in an outer-space simulation for seventy-two hours. The students would then carry out the three-day mission and wrap it up with a final evaluation of the project. The result of the considerable change in the curriculum for the architecture students was Project Space Station.

After the success of Project Space Station, the technical drafting students wanted to get involved. The space station needed an orbital maneu-vering vehicle (OMV) with mechanical or robotic arms to launch satellites and do repairs. The technical drafting students then had a part to play in the project; they took on the task of designing and building the OMV. Soon, the metal technology students developed and produced containers to hold experiments, food and clothing.

Students from other classes were quick to get involved with the project and were asking how they could contribute. About four hundred students worked on many components of the space station. The McCullough Students Astronauts club (McCSA) was originated to help consolidate the efforts of the many students.

Soon the whole school was involved in Project Space Station. The food-services classes researched space food and then precooked and packaged all the meals for the astronauts. Physics classes helped build robotic arms; language arts students prepared the astronauts for all the writing that would be required; social-studies classes took an active part in soliciting support and participation from local, state, and national elected officials. Before long, the community had also come out to participate, donating money, materials, or discounts on needed items. Professional mentorships and job opportunities were made available to students.

Today the Central Project is an established part of the Conroe High School curriculum. Teachers guide students through the Central Project theme with corresponding lessons that relate to the Central Project. Research papers; math projects; science experiments; social-studies activities; art, drama and musical presentations; and vocational projects all pertain to some aspect of the Central Project. Decorations and exhibits in the hall, on bulletin boards, in classrooms, and even the cafeteria shout messages relating to the Central Project.

Like any major undertaking in the business world, Central Projects are usually too large and intricate for any one person or class to complete and must be broken down into smaller, individual or group projects called Component Projects. Some component projects are divided again into sub-components. It is in this division of labor that students learn to work in teams and consolidate their efforts in a complex organization.

One of the chief stated purposes for Conroe High School is to become an intellectual incubator where students learn how to learn and thus to teach themselves. The goal is for students to leave McCullough High equipped with the ability and desire to become lifelong learners. The Central Project, with its ability to capture students' imagination and to let them work in a "real" environment, is proving a highly effective means to that end.

Schools Within Schools[10]

George Westinghouse High School in Chicago, Illinois, traditionally known as a vocational high school, has made a commitment to achieve a more effective integration of hands-on vocational study with solid academic content and skills. Their aim is to produce students who not only are equipped to compete successfully in the world of work, but who also have more choices about working and/or going to college after high school. To this end, administrators are supporting and encouraging both strong academics and strong occupational education—and close integration between the two.

The English department, for example, builds some of its activities on career-related vocabulary words supplied by teachers of occupational courses. Some courses are specifically designed to incorporate two or more different disciplines. The City Experience class, which focuses on Chicago's distinctive and world-famous architecture, features a successful merging of English and architectural drafting disciplines. Students speak and write about the topic of Chicago architecture in the classroom. They also take field trips to see the architecture firsthand and keep journals and reports from these trips.

But Westinghouse's commitment to integrating academic content with hands-on application and vocational emphasis goes much deeper than the design of a few classes. Westinghouse is working to reorganize the entire curriculum. Called Westinghouse Tech Prep (WTP, or Tech Prep), the new structure is designed to combine a significant amount of academic knowledge with applied career training.

Prep Tech consists of three major instructional clusters, or "schools within a school" organized around different groups of related occupational areas. Each school enrolls about five hundred students and shares a staff of about thirty teachers. To facilitate integration of academic study with work-related study, the teaching teams include both academic and career-related faculty.

The first school-within-a-school, the School of Commerce and Communication, groups teachers of academic classes with teachers for the areas of business, architectural drafting, commercial art, and printing. The School of Professional Services includes an academic staff plus teachers of cosmetology, fashion design, culinary arts, and health careers. The School of Evolving Technologies teams an academic staff with teachers of automotive services, building trades, electronics, and manufacturing systems.

Houses of Learning[11]

Another version of the "schools within a school" idea has helped transform John Marshall High School in Los Angeles, California. John Marshall High has made a special effort to get parents and the community involved in school-based management, to improve efficiency in the use of resources using private-industry standards and techniques, and to link the school more closely to area agencies, businesses, and industry. Along with these innovations has come a restructuring; the students and staff are grouped into smaller units or "houses" of learning.

Each house of learning at John Marshall High consists of a group of teachers and counselors and a defined group of students. Teachers, counselors, and students (and their parents) will stay in the same house of learning throughout high school. In all the houses of learning, and in all subjects, special emphasis is placed on critical-thinking skills, problem solving, and decision making. Parental involvement is also stressed; parents now have at least two meetings a year with their students' school counselors and teachers.

School for the Sky[12]

At Aviation High School in New York City, students get a chance to specialize in aviation mechanics and careers relating to engineering while receiving a solid academic education. Upon graduation, students have the opportunity to receive various aviation-related diplomas and certificates from New York State, New York City, the Federal Aviation Agency (FAA), and the Federal Communications Commission (FCC). Or they can choose to go on to college, working toward either a regular baccalaureate degree at a four-year college or an associate degree at a community or technical college. A local community college has articulated its two-year aeronautics program with the program so that students may attend both the high school classes and those at the community college.

As in most exemplary schools, the attendance rate for this public high school is much higher and the dropout rate is much lower than those for most schools in the New York City School system. More than 95% of the students graduate. A peer tutoring program is available for those students falling behind.

Several factors contribute to Aviation High School's remarkable success:
1. The purposes of the school are clear and permeate the whole organization.
2. It is one of the few high schools certified by the FAA.
3. It prepares students well in the academic areas so that college is also a viable choice.
4. It provides students with career connections that easily translate into job offers.
5. It has an atmosphere that is safe, free of crime and delinquency, and conducive to learning.

Close ties between the school and business community help ensure the recognition of Aviation graduates. All major airlines and the Grumman Corporation maintain contact with Aviation High through the school's Aeronautics Advisory Board. This board also acts as a sort of quality-control body, making sure that the subject matter and skills taught at Aviation are the ones most needed in aviation.

A Tech Prep Transformation[13]

Chopticon High School has demonstrated some amazing student success for all students by installing a schoolwide contextual-learning program which includes, tech prep and university prep components. According to former principal Stephen Olczak, faculty and administration made the decision to eliminate the so-called general education track entirely and replace it with a closely focused tech prep program.

The Chopticon High School requires the following of all its students:

1. *Every student must select a clear focus or major for his or her high school study and then relate all his or her course taking to that major.* The potluck approach to student course selection has been eliminated. Students are not locked in to a single course of study, but they must choose one with which to start.

2. *Every student must develop an individual learning plan that also contains a destination following high school*—whether to work, a community college, or a four-year college. (Again, there is plenty of room for change, but students must start out with a plan.) For those who want to earn an associate degree, the path has been smoothed by a carefully designed articulation plan with the nearby Charles County Community College. Some students may earn college credit while in high school, but the major purpose of this articulation is to ensure that students are able to progress smoothly from high school to college with a minimum of backtracking, remediation, or redundancy.

3. *Every student must reach for high standards.* The faculty have developed high expectations for all students, but they have gone beyond high expectations to developing applied-learning programs that help students *meet* those high expectations.

What has been the result of this education reform effort? One measure of success is the performance of Chopticon students on the Maryland School Performance Program, which indicates student achievement:

- The pass rate on the Maryland functional math achievement test for Chopticon students jumped from 65 percent in the 1988-89 school year to 84 percent in the 1992-93 school year.
- The pass rate on the writing test increased from 75 percent in 1988-89 to 96 percent in the 1992-93 school year.
- The pass rate on the citizenship test climbed from 60 percent in 1988-89 to 86 percent in 1992-93.
- The four-year high school dropout rate plunged from 32 percent to 6 percent over the same four-year period.

Test scores aren't everything, of course, but these scores fully support the observations of students, faculty, administration, and parents at Chopticon High School. All agree that improvement has been marked. Faculty member Joe Baker states unequivocally, "We [the faculty] have proven to ourselves that our students learn more quickly and retain more knowledge if taught using the applied-learning methods."

A Pioneer Partnership[14]

In Richmond County, North Carolina a pioneer partnership has been forged between a high school and a community college. Richmond High School, under the leadership of principal Ralph Robertson and superintendent Douglas James, has joined hands with Richmond Community College, under the leadership of college president Joe Grimsley, to develop a Tech Prep/Associate Degree program that is now one of the longest-running articulated programs of its type in the country.

Superintendent James indicates that the program has had the greatest impact on secondary education in Richmond County of anything since high schools were consolidated in 1971. The high school dropout rate has dropped dramatically. In addition, more students are taking math and science classes and experiencing more success. The community college also reports significant improvements since the institution of the tech prep program. Enrollment of recent high school graduates has shown a significant increase. More important, these students are better prepared academically than ever before.

EXEMPLARY PRACTICES IN POSTSECONDARY EDUCATION

Rethinking the Future[15]

Tacoma Community College in Tacoma, Washington offers a unique interdisciplinary course for studying trends, challenges, and opportunities that will affect the work environment in the twenty-first century. The course is called Rethinking the Future. Launched in 1989 under the leadership of professors Bob Thaden and John Geubtner (with input from students and the business community), this course was designed to help students

- understand diverse issues that cross subject-matter boundaries,
- enjoy the experience of participating in an interactive learning situation,
- integrate course content with practice in writing skills,
- improve in the ability to inquire and to think analytically.

Ten college credits may be earned for completion of the course, which runs two hours per day, five days a week. Enrollment is limited to fifty students per quarter.

Although content and skills from many different disciplines find their way into the Rethinking the Future curriculum, business and English composition are the primary components of the course. The purpose for the combination is to help students enhance their written and oral communication abilities, understand key business concepts, learn college-level outlining skills, and apply paragraph-writing techniques to business issues and topics.

When it comes to teaching methods, Rethinking the Future leaves tradition far behind. There are no textbooks. Instead, as an example, the *Wall Street Journal* is a staple resource. Students follow certain columns such as "What's News," as well as the Marketplace section and the international pages, to stay on top of industry changes and spot developing trends. In addition to keeping up with the *Journal,* students read the daily local paper, review *Wall Street Journal Reports,* and analyze other resources. As a result, "Students are exposed to 'real world' situations. They are challenged to test hypotheses, explore alternatives, and reach their own conclusions."

Tacoma Community College president Ray Needham says this course has been highly successful in a number of ways. Students not only have increased their knowledge and skills, they became "turned on" to learning. The faculty at TCC have become excited about the innovative interdisciplinary and team approach to teaching and have begun thinking about testing the waters themselves. Business leaders have communicated their pleasure with the program to the students, faculty, and other business leaders.

Making the Most of ASSETS[16]

A cooperative effort between an employer and a community college has given students in Gresham, Oregon the opportunity to learn theory and apply workplace skills at the same time. Ford Motor Company linked up with Mt. Hood Community College (MHCC) in a program called ASSET (Automotive Student Service Educational Training). Its purpose is to educate and give technical training to future automotive service technicians for Ford dealerships.

The two-year ASSET program alternates classroom and laboratory instruction every other term with actual work experience at Ford dealerships or at the new Ford Corporate Service Training Center on the MHCC campus. This system offers ASSET students free access to state-of-the-art equipment, technical information, training aids, specialty tools, and manuals as well as giving them the opportunity to experience what they learn in class. Ford has also installed a satellite dish at MHCC with a downlink from the Ford Motor Company Communication System, allowing participants in both the on-site and the off-site programs to teleconference, update technology, and share information.

The ASSET program is an outstanding example of possibilities inherent in a business-education partnership. It is not the *only* example, however. General Motors and Chrysler have developed similar programs in cooperation with many other community colleges across the country, with similar salutary results.

A New Perspective on Physics[17]

Undergraduate physics students at the United States Air Force Academy, Colorado Springs, Colorado, are looking at problem solving from a new perspective. Instead of suffering from the passive learning syndrome, they are learning to play an active role in their own educations. In the physics department's senior seminars, collaborative learning techniques and student competition are being used to motivate and involve students in solving real-life problems. Seminar participants are divided into teams and challenged with problems that force them to call on several different physics concepts they have learned. Team members work together to solve the problems and present their solutions to the class, striving to earn points for various aspects of their work and thereby beat their competition.

Lieutenant Colonel John C. Souders, Jr., who teaches in the physics department, reports that this interactive approach to physics seminars has paid multiple benefits. Students enjoy the challenge and the teamwork and become more actively involved in learning. Many students also report that the seminars help prepare them for postgraduate interviews. And faculty members enjoy the seminars because working with an involved and enthusiastic group of problem solvers is always more fun than lecturing to a roomful of bored and passive note takers.

Applied Academics Take Off with Boeing[18]

The Boeing Company has provided leadership and funding for an unprecedented partnership with Washington area colleges and high schools as well. This effort began in the late 1980s when Boeing conducted several studies on the competencies of their job applicants and entry-level workers. They recognized a sizable mismatch between the needs of a high-performance work organization and the skills the applicants were bringing to the jobs. Many showed deficiencies in mathematics, communications (including reading and writing), and problem-solving skills (the ability to apply knowledge).

In 1990, in response to these studies, Boeing Company officials commissioned a company task force to meet with education leaders to determine how the nation's largest aerospace corporation might help schools and colleges better prepare students for the workplace. The task force concluded that Boeing could use its influence as a major national employer, to convince state and local policy makers of the benefits of applied academics. In addition, they could offer money to help teachers and school systems develop applied-academics courses and train teachers in applied-learning techniques. Boeing president Frank Shrontz, senior vice president Deone Cruze, and corporate director Carver Gayton agreed that a significant investment of company profits in applied academics would have a long-term payoff not only for Boeing, but for employers throughout the nation.

Since then, many high schools and colleges across the Northwest have been the beneficiaries of Boeing dollars aimed at integrating academic and vocational education. Summer internships, for example, have helped teachers overhaul courses and develop applied-learning course modules.

Then, in spring of 1993, Boeing initiated a tech prep intern program. Five students from five high schools and two faculty members from each school were selected as tech prep interns and worked together through the month of July with pay in a carefully planned sequence of experiences. The students then committed to a four-year sequence of study combining two years of high school with two years in a community college and culminating with an associate degree in manufacturing technology. Boeing aims at involving 250-300 students and faculty annually in this program. They want to demonstrate how a tech prep program can combine academics with work-based learning to bring about significantly improved teaching and learning in the applied mode.

PACE Setters in South Carolina[19]

Tri-County Technical College, under the leadership of its president, Don Garrison, has developed a consortium of schools, college, and university aimed at implementing a Tech Prep/Associate Degree program. Known as PACE (Partnership for Academic and Career Education), this consortium endeavors to eliminate curricular gaps and overlaps between secondary and postsecondary levels of education as well as implementing and administering the tech prep program at all levels of education.

A key component of the PACE program at the secondary school is an emphasis on using applied-learning techniques to build a stronger academic foundation for all students. The clear result has been a reduced need for developmental or remedial education programs at the postsecondary level. Students are finding it easier to transition smoothly from one level of education to the next step—and thus are motivated to take that next step.

A New Approach to Calculus[20]

A grant from the National Science Foundation has allowed students in Washington State to experience a new way of learning calculus. Instead of doing their homework alone, students involved in the statewide Calculus Dissemination Project discuss their math problems in a group.

This approach is based on the theory that learning is a social activity. "Students learn much better by talking about the problem with others, as opposed to going home and staring at a wall at night," says Robert Cole, who spearheads the project at Evergreen State University in Olympia. In addition to the collaborative-learning approach, the classes of the Calculus Dissemination Project stress active learning, writing and talking, applications, and technology. Students apply their skills to engaging, real-world problems and make extensive use of calculators, computers, and other technological aids.

College students and faculty across the state are excited about the possibilities of the program. In autumn of 1993, 30 percent of calculus students in Washington were taking the course, with twenty colleges and universities participating. Plans are being made to involve fifteen more schools in the near future.

SCANNING FOR A MORE EFFECTIVE WORKFORCE

Even though the Secretary's Commission on Achieving Necessary Skills (SCANS) is not exactly an exemplary practice in a school or college, the reports of this important Commission[21] represent some exemplary recommendations that relate directly to our LogoLearning thesis of integrating information or content with the context of application.

The SCANS group was formed in 1989 under the leadership of then Secretary of Labor Elizabeth Dole and Assistant Secretary Roberts Jones. Representatives from business, industry, labor, government, and education labored mightily to shed light on the question: What does work require of schools? (This was also the title of the first Commission Report, which was issued in 1991.)

Commission members and staff interviewed more than a thousand private and public employers to discover what they currently expect from educational institutions and what they would require in the future. As a result of extensive research and discussion, the Commission formulated a set of recommendations for schools, listing the skills and qualities were boiled down to a three part foundation involving — basic skills, personal qualities, and a five part set of workplace competencies that employers wish schools would foster in future workers (see table 1).

CLASSROOM ASSIGNMENTS THAT INTREGRATE THE SCANS COMPETENCIES INTO THE CORE CURRICULUM AREA

Competencies	English/Writing	Mathematics	Science	Social Studies/ Geography	History
			CURRICULUM AREA		
Resources	Write a proposal for an after-school career lecture series that schedules speakers, coordinates audiovisual aids, and estimates costs.	Develop a monthly family budget, taking into account expenses and revenues, and – using information from the budget plan – schedule a vacation trip that stays within the resources available.	Plan the material and time requirements for a chemistry experiment, to be performed over a two-day period, that demonstrates a natural growth process in terms of resource needs.	Design a chart of resource needs for a community of African Zulus. Analyze the reasons three major cities grew to their current size.	Study the Vietnam War, researching and making an oral presentation on the timing and logistics of transport of materials and troops to Vietnam and on the impact of the war on the federal budget.
Interpersonal Skills	Discuss the pros and cons of the argument that Shakespeare's Merchant of Venice is a racist play and should be banned from the school curriculum.	Present the results of a survey to the class, and justify the use of specific statistics to analyze and represent the data.	Work in a group to design an experiment to analyze the lead content in the school's water. Teach the results to an elementary school class.	In front of a peer panel, debate whether to withdraw U.S. military support from Japan. Simulate an urban planning exercise for Paris.	Study America's Constitution and roleplay negotiation of the wording of the free state/slave state clause by different signers.
Information	Identify and abstract passage from a novel to support an assertion about the values of a key character	Design and carry out a survey, analyzing data in a spreadsheet program using algebraic formulas. Develop table and graphic display to communicate results.	In an entrepreneurship project, present statistical data on a high-tech company's production/sales. Use computer to develop statistical charts.	Using numerical data and charts, develop and present conclusions about the effects of economic conditions on the quality of life in several countries.	Research and present papers on effects of the Industrial Revolution on class structure in Britain, citing data sources used in drawing conclusions.

134

CURRICULUM AREA					
Competencies	English/Writing	Mathematics	Science	Social Studies/ Geography	History
Systems	Develop a computer model that analyzes the motivation of Shakespeare's Hamlet. Plot the events that increase Hamlet's motivation to avenge the death of his father by killing Claudius.	Develop a system, to monitor and correct the heating/cooling process in a computer laboratory, using principles of statistical control.	Build a model of human population growth that includes the impact of the amount of food available on birth and death rates, etc. Do the same for a growth model for insects.	Analyze the accumulation of capital in industrialized nations in systems terms (as a reinforcing process with stocks and flows).	Develop a model of the social forces that led to the American Revolution. Then explore the fit between that model and other revolutions.
Technology	Write an article showing the relationship between technology and the environment. Use word processing to write and edit papers after receiving teacher feedback.	Read manuals for several data-processing programs and write a memo recommending the best programs to handle a series of mathematical situations.	Calibrate a scale to weigh accurate portions of chemicals for an experiment. Trace the development of this technology from earliest uses to today.	Research and report on the development and functions of the seismograph and its role in earthquake prediction and detection.	Analyze the effects of wars on technological development. Use computer graphics to plot the relationship of the country's economic growth to periods of peace and war.

Source: *Teaching the SCANS Competencies* (1992), *The Secretary's Commission on Achieving Necessary Skills, U.S. Department of Labor.* *This document is for sale by the U.S. Government Printing Office ISBN 0-16-037908-3.*

THE FOUNDATION
Competence requires:
- **Basic Skills:** reading, writing, arithmetic and mathematics, speaking and listening.
- **Thinking Skills:** thinking creatively, making decisions, solving problems, seeing things in the mind's eye, knowing how to learn, and reasoning.
- **Personal Qualities:** individual responsibility, self-esteem, sociability, self-management and integrity.

WORKPLACE COMPETENCIES
Effective workers can productively use:
- **Resources:** allocating time, money, materials, space, staff.
- **Interpersonal Skills:** working on teams, teaching others, serving customers, leading, negotiating, and working well with people from culturally diverse backgrounds.
- **Information:** acquiring and evaluating data, organizing and maintaining files, interpreting and communicating, and using computers to process information.
- **Systems:** understanding social, organizational, and technological systems, monitoring and correcting performance, and designing or improving systems.
- **Technology:** selecting equipment and tools, applying technology to specific tasks, and maintaining and troubleshooting technologies.

Contextual learning is the underlying premise of the SCANS recommendations. This Commission was unanimous in its belief that learning to know must be integrated with learning to do in the classrooms of America. Commissioners were quick to point out, however, that classrooms must be places for learning and not simulated worksites. There is and must be much more to the education experience than simply preparing individuals for the life role of work. Still, work represents a touchstone of reality for nearly everyone, and the need for occupational preparedness is a motivational factor in personal or national economic life in a rapidly changing world.

----

[1] "First Grade in Wisconsin," *Better Homes and Gardens*, February 1993, 35.

[2] Alan Deutschman, "Why Kids Should Learn About Work," *Fortune*, 10 August 1992, 87.

[3] For more information about this program contact Sally Leet, Principal, Ardenwald Elementary School or Elizabeth Gill, Principal, Seth Lewelling Elementary School in Milwaukie, OR 97222.

[4] Jay La Gregs, "Some Relationships Just Work Right," *The Apache* campus newsletter for Tyler Junior College, Fall 1993, 13–16.

[5] Kari Hulai, "Oregon Schools Try Putting Emphasis on Real World Skills," *The Oregonian*, 23 November 1993, B2.

[6] For information on the Weather Satellite Program contact Clear Choice Educational Products in Helm, GA.

[7] For information on the development of the Compact Disc Interactive (CD-I) contact Bernard Luskin, President of Phillips Interactive Media in Los Angeles, CA.

[8] Tamara Henry, "Giving Math a Meaning That Motivates," *USA Today*, 15 September 1993. For more information contact Patricia Aramendia, Principal, Mission High School, San Francisco, CA.

[9] For more information contact Larry J. McHaney or L. Jerry Bernhardt Jr., Mc Cullough High School, 3800 S. Panther Creek Drive, The Woodlands, TX 77381.

[10] For more information contact Stanton P. Payne, Principal, George Westinghouse High School, 3301 West Franklin Boulevard, Chicago, IL 60624.

[11] For more information contact Barbara Knight, Counselor, John Marcshall High School, 3939 Tracy Street, Los Angeles, CA 90027.

[12] For more information contact David P. Ramos, Assistant Principal, Aviation High School, Queens Boulevard, End 36th Street, Long Island City, NY 11101.

[13] For more information on the Chopticon High School program contact Stephen Olczak, Principal, Supervisor, Career and Technology Education, St. Mary's County Technical Center, Leonardtown, MD 20650.

[14] For more information contact Douglas James, Superintendent, Richmond County Schools, Hamlet, NC 28345.

[15] For more information contact Ray Needham, President, Tacoma Community College, Tacoma, WA 98465.

[16] For more information contact Paul Kreider, President, Mt. Hood Community College, Gresham, OR 97030.

[17] John C. Souders, Jr., "Problem-Solving Teams in Undergraduate Physics Seminars," *College Teaching*, Summer 1991, 108.

[18] Thomas Owens, "The Boeing Company Applied Academics," October 1992. For more information on the Boeing project contact Carver Gayton, Corporate Director, College and University Relations, The Boeing Company, Seattle, WA 98124 or Richard Lengyel, Tech Prep Administrator, Boeing Commercial Airplane Group, Seattle, WA 98124-2207.

[19] For more information contact Diane Walter, Executive Director, PACE., P.O. Box 587, Pendleton, SC.

[20] "Calculus Dissemination Project," *Greener Scene/Happenings: The Newsletter of the Evergreen State College*, 12 November 1993, 1.

[21] The following publications were all produced by The Secretary's Commission on Achieving Necessary Skills, United States Department of Labor, and were printed in Washington, D.C. by the Government Printing Office: *What Work Requires of Schools: A SCANS Report for America 2000* (1992), *Skills and Tasks for JOBS* (1992), *Learning a Living: A Blueprint for High Performance* (1992), *Teaching the SCANS Competencies* (1993).

[22] Source: The Secretary's Commission, *What Work Requires of Schools*.

[23] Source: The Secretary's Commission, *Teaching the SCANS Competencies*. This document is for sale by the Government Printing Office, Washington, D.C. 20402-9328. Ask for ISBN 0-16-037908-3

Epilogue
Some Afterthoughts

In writing a book like this, one becomes increasingly aware of one's own limited knowledge and the vast amount of research and knowledge yet to be uncovered. Even in this scientific age, we still know so little about the brain and how people learn. No attempt has been made in this book to be inclusive of pedagogical history or research. Rather, my purpose has been to shine the floodlights on the process of teaching and learning for meaning.

Excellence in education will not be achieved by political pronouncements or by pompous pontification from those who have never experienced teaching in the classroom. It will be achieved only as classroom instructors at all levels of education lead the way. Well-trained teachers and support staff are the heart of an excellent education system, and schools and colleges can develop meaningful learning for students only as classroom leaders envision and practice teaching for meaning. This will require an investment in teacher training and staff development. Unfortunately, this is often one of the first items cut in budget reduction exercises.

Teachers have a heavy responsibility to help students see meaning in their educational program. If students are to be motivated to learn, they must know why they are learning, how this learning connects with other learning, and where this learning intersects with real-life experiences. Keeping this "why" at the forefront of education requires a continuous effort to improve the way we teach and the way we structure our curricula.

Something else must come first, however. If we want instructors to be highly motivated to teach, administrators motivated to lead, school board members and college trustees motivated to develop wise policies, and the public motivated to support our schools and colleges, we must pay unrelenting attention to purposes. These purposes must be developed with such precision and with such power and clarity that all involved will be able to develop a sense of personal meaning and commitment to them. As much or more attention must be given to purposes than is now is being given to anticipated outcomes. Clear and understandable statements of purpose for a school system or a curricular course or an individual lesson are absolutely essential to achieving excellence in education.

All of this requires an unprecedented amount of good communication among teachers and between teachers, administrators, and support staff about the meat and potatoes of education called teaching and learning. Competition must give way to cooperation up and down the line in educational organizations. People working together with shared values and purposes are the beginning of excellence in education. As Roland Barth writes

The relationships among the adults in schools are the basis, the precondition, the sine qua non that allow, energize, and sustain all other attempts at school improvement. Unless adults talk with one another, observe one another, and help one another, very little will change."[1]

Emphasis upon the extrinsic motivations of numerical goals, tests, records, ratings, and punishments will not bring excellence, only conformance. We must not lose touch with the fact that true change is internal; it is intrinsic motivation that really drives people. We must seek change and personal transformation in students (and in teachers) so that they find meaning and purpose in education and consequently in life.

As the biblical sign over the church nursery door put it, "We shall not all sleep, but we shall all be changed"(1 Corinthians 15:51).

A FINAL OBSERVATION

As a long-time educator, I understand the often conflicting demands made upon our schools and our colleges and especially on our teachers. There is much special pleading for one special interest or another, and every innovation seems to bring more work, more criticism, and more paperwork. Yet I write without reservation to urge change in the name of LogoLearning because I write on behalf of the student, our most important national resource.

We must provide all our students with meaningful education experiences that will help all students move into the economic mainstream of American life. We cannot afford to leave anyone behind if we can help it. We must help all students develop the competencies (knowledge, skills, values) required to be lifelong learners, thinking workers, discerning citizens, wise consumers, responsible family members, and participants in the aesthetic aspects of life.

Educators all across America have accepted the challenge and are seizing the moment. They are choosing hope over hopelessness, opportunity over oppression, wisdom over waste, and meaning over mindlessness. Indeed, it is this kind of education that is our last and best hope for our nation. We must never give up on our noble calling.

---

[1] Roland S. Barth, *Improving Schools from Within: Teachers, Parents, and Principals Can Make A Difference* (San Francisco: Jossey-Bass, 1990), 32.

Appendix
A LogoLearning Teaching Evaluation Form

Student evaluation is a fact of life in many schools. Evaluation is appropriately used as a teaching tool and to provide feedback for teachers as to how well they are reaching students. In my observation, however, many standard evaluation forms do not address the critical issues of teaching and learning. With that in mind, I have developed a LogoLearning-based evaluation form to serve as an example of how a more useful evaluation form might be developed.

LOGOLEARNING STUDENT EVALUATION FORM

Please mark your responses according to the following rating scale:

5 = strongly agree
4 = agree
3 = tend to agree
2 = tend to disagree
1 = strongly disagree
N/A = does not apply

_____1. Classroom Performance
   A. The teacher provided a good mix of knowing and doing activities.
   B. The students were actively involved in the learning process.
   C. Videotapes, visual aids, and simulation activities were on target and beneficial.

_____2. Content and Context
   A. The content of the class was relevant, practical, and useful to my present or future career or personal life.
   B. The content was presented within the context of application.

_____3. Conformance
   A. The established goals for the course were related to overall institutional purpose.
   B. The teacher followed the course syllabus and outline.

_____4. Caring
   A. The teacher was available to me and to other students.
   B. The teacher cared about students' success.
   C. I was satisfied with the formality (or lack of formality) in this class.

_____ 5. Current
  A. The teacher seemed to stay abreast of current scholarly developments and incorporated useful new knowledge into the course.
  B. What I learned in this class will be of long-term value to me.

_____ 6. This course helped me acquire new knowledge.

_____ 7. This course helped me understand how to apply my new knowledge.

_____ 8. This course helped me assimilate my new knowledge into my thinking for future use.

_____ 9. This course helped me associate my new knowledge with the process of problem solving.

_____ 10. Class Quality
  A. In comparison with other courses of a similar nature that you have taken, how would you rate your level of learning in this course?
  _____a) I learned a great deal more than I usually do.
  _____b) I learned more than I usually do.
  _____c) I learned about as much as I usually do.
  _____d) I learned less than I usually do.
  _____e) I learned considerably less than I usually do.

Can you develop two or three ideas that you believe would have made this course more useful to you?

Bibliography

Aldridge, W. *Essential Changes In Secondary School Science: Scope, Sequence, and Coordination.* Washington, D.C.: National Science Teachers Association, 1989.

Applebee, Arthur, Judith Langen, and Ina V. S. Mullis. *Crossroads in American Education.* Princeton, N.J.: Educational Testing Service, 1989.

Bailey, Thomas, and Sue Berryman. *The Double Helix of Education and the Economy.* New York: Institute in Education and the Economy, Columbia University, 1992.

Barth, Roland S. *Improving Schools from Within: Teachers, Parents, and Principals Can Make A Difference.* San Francisco: Jossey-Bass, 1990.

Benjamin, Harold. *The Saber-Tooth Curriculum.* New York: McGraw-Hill, 1939.

Bennet, E. L., M. C. Diamond, D. Knech, and M. R. Rozensweig. "Chemical and Anatomical Plasticity of the Brain." *Science,* 146 (1964): 610–619.

"First Grade in Wisconsin," *Better Homes and Gardens,* February 1993.

Bloom, Benjamin S. *All Our Children Learning.* New York: McGraw-Hill, 1981.

_____, ed. *Taxonomy of Educational Objectives Handbook: Cognitive Domain.* New York: McKay, 1956.

Boorstin, Daniel. *The Image: A Guide to Pseudo Events in America.* New York: Macmillan, 1988.

Bottoms, Gene, Alice Presson, and Mary Johnson. *Making High Schools Work.* Atlanta: Southern Regional Education Board, 1992.

Boyer, Ernest. *A Quest for Common Learning.* Princeton: Carnegie Foundation for the Advancement of Teaching, Princeton University Press.

Bransford, John., et al. "New Approaches to Instruction: Because Wisdom Can't Be Told." In *Similarity and Analytical Reasonings.* Cambridge: Cambridge University Press, 1989.

Bridges, Edwin M. *Problem Based Learning for Administrators.* Eugene: University of Oregon, ERIC Clearinghouse on Educational Management, 1992.

Brown, J. S., A. Collins, and P. Duquid. "Situated Cognition and the Culture of Learning," *Educational Researcher* 18, no. 1 (1989): 32–41.

Bruner, Jerome S., I. J. Goodnow, and G.A. Austin. *A Study of Thinking.* New York: Science Editions, 1962.

_____. *Toward a Theory of Instruction.* Cambridge: Harvard University Press, 1966.

Caine, Renate Numella and Geoffrey Caine. *Making Connections: Teaching and the Human Brain.* Alexandria: Association for Supervision and Curriculum Development, 1991.

Clinchy, Evans. "Needed: A Clinton Crusade for Quality and Equality." *Phi Delta Kappan,* April 1993, 607.

Cohen, Audrey. "A New Educational Paradigm," *Phi Delta Kappan,* June 1993, 793.

Coleman, James S. "The Children Have Outgrown the Schools," *Psychology Today,* February 1972, 72–84.

Cowan, P. A. *Piaget with Feeling: Cognitive, Social, and Emotional Dimensions.* New York: Holt, Rinehart and Winston, 1978.

Dempster, Frank. "Exposing Our Students to Less Should Help Them Learn More," *Phi Delta Kappan,* February 1993, 433–437, 87.

Deutschman, Alan. "Why Kids Should Learn About Work," *Fortune*, 10 August 1992.

Dewey, John. "Morals and Conduct." In *The World's Great Thinkers: The Social Philosophers*. New York: Random House, 1947 .

_____. *The Ingles Lecture*. Cambridge: Harvard University Press, 1931.

Dickston, Douglas. "The Pen Pal Letter: A Separate Audience." *Innovation Abstracts* 15, no. 23 (1993).

Diamond, M. *Enriching Heredity: The Impact of the Environment on the Anatomy of the Brain*. New York: Free Press, 1988.

Farnham-Diggory, Sylvia. *Cognitive Processes in Education*. New York: Harper-Collins, 1992.

Frankl, Viktor. *Man's Search for Meaning: An Introduction to Logotherapy*. Translated by Ilse Lasch. Boston: Beacon, 1963.

_____. *The Unheard Cry for Meaning*. New York: Simon and Schuster, 1978.

Freire, Paulo. *Pedagogy of the Oppressed*. New York: Seaview, 1971.

Gabor, A. *The Man Who Discovered Quality*. New York: Penguin, 1990.

Gardner, H. *Frames of Mind: The Theory of Multiple Intelligence*. New York: Basic Books, 1985.

_____. *Frames of Mind: The Theory of Multiple Intelligence*. 10th anniversary edition. New York: Basic Books, 1985.

_____. *The Unschooled Mind*. New York: Basic Books, 1991.

_____. "Beyond the IQ: Education and Human Development," *Phi Kappa Phi Journal*, Spring 1988.

Gentile, Ronald J. *Instructional Improvement: Summary of Analysis of Madeline Hunter's Essential Elements of Instruction and Supervision*. Oxford: National Staff Development Council, 1988.

Gibbons, Maurice. "Walkabout: Searching for the Right Passage from Childhood and School." *Phi Delta Kappan*, May 1974, 596–602.

Goldhammer, Keith, and Robert Taylor. *Career Education: Perspective and Promise*. New York: Charles E. Merrill, 1972.

Goleman, David. "Rethinking the Value of Intelligence Tests." *New York Times Supplement*, 9 November 1986.

Graves, Bill. "Student Cheating," *The Oregonian*, 21 October 1993.

Hechinger, Fred M. "School-College Collaboration—An Essential to Improved Public Education." *National Association of Secondary School Principals Bulletin*, October 1984, 69–79.

Henry, Tamara. "Giving Math a Meaning That Motivates," *USA Today*, 15 September 1993.

Horvath, Frank. "Many Kids Fall Below Standard," *Calgary Herald*. 11 November 1993.

Hulai, Kari. "Oregon Schools Try Putting Emphasis On Real World Skills" *The Oregonian*, 23 November 1993, B2.

Hull, Dan. *Opening Minds, Opening Doors: The Rebirth of American Education*. Waco: Center for Occupational Research and Development, 1993.

Hull, Dan, and Dale Parnell eds. *Tech Prep Associate Degree: A Win/Win Experience*. Waco: Center for Occupational Research and Development, 1991.

James, William. *Talks to Teachers on Psychology*. New York: W. W. Norton, 1958.

Johnson-Laird, P. N. *The Computer and the Mind: An Introduction to Cognitive Science*. Cambridge: Harvard University Press, 1988.

La Gregs, Jay. "Some Relationships Just Work Right." *The Apache* campus newsletter for Tyler Junior College, Tyler, Fall 1993.

MacLean, P. D. *A Mind of Three Minds: Educating the Triune Brain.* Chicago: University of Chicago Press, 1978.

Maslow, Abraham. *Motivation and Personality.* New York: Harper & Row, 1954.

Ornstein, R., and F. F. Thompson. *The Amazing Brain.* Boston: Houghton Mifflin, 1984.

Owens, Thomas. *The Boeing Company Applied Academics.* Evaluation report published by Northwest Regional Educational Laboratory, Portland, Oregon, 1992.

Parnell, Dale. *Dateline 2000: The New Higher Education Agenda.* Washington: Community College Press, 1990.

_____. *The Neglected Majority.* Washington: Community College Press, 1985.

_____. "The Oregon Walkabout." *Phi Delta Kappan,* November 1974, 205–206.

People for the American Way. *Democracy's Next Generation.* Washington: People for the American Way, 1989.

Peronne, Vito. *Portraits of High Schools.* Princeton: Carnegie Foundation for the Advancement of Teaching, Princeton University Press, 1985.

Postman, Neil, and C. Weingartner. *Teaching As a Subversive Activity.* New York: Dell, 1969.

Press, Pat. "It's Not Dirty Work," *Washington Post,* 27 May 1984.

Raywid, Mary Anne. *The Ax-Grinders.* New York: Macmillan, 1963.

Resnick, Lauren. "Learning In School and Out," *Educational Researcher,* December 1987, 13–20.

Raspberry, William. "Best U.S. Students Test Well Against Other Nations." *Washington Post,* 16 October 1993.

Rosenthal, Robert, and Lenore Jacobsen. *Pygmalion in the Classroom.* New York: Holt, Rinehart and Winston, 1992.

Sizer, Theodore B. *Horace's Compromise: The Dilemma of the American High School Today.* Boston: Houghton Mifflin, 1984.

Stepien, William, and Shelagh Gallagher. "Problem-Based Learning: As Authentic As It Gets," *Educational Leadership,* April 1993.

Sternberg, Robert. *The Triarchic Mind: A New Theory of Human Intelligence.* New York: Viking, 1988.

Stigler, James W., and Harold W. Stevenson. "How Asian Teachers Polish Each Lesson to Perfection." *American Federation of Teachers Journal,* Spring 1991.

Swinton's Third Grade Readers. New York: American Book Company, 1882.

United States Department of Education. *America 2000: An Education Strategy Sourcebook.* Washington: U.S. Government Printing Office, 1992.

United States Department of Labor, Secretary's Commission on Achieving Necessary Skills. *Learning a Living: A Blueprint for High Performance.* Washington: U.S. Government Printing Office, 1992.

_____. *Skills and Tasks for JOBS.* Washington: U.S. Government Printing Office, 1992.

_____. *Teaching the SCANS Competencies,* Washington: U.S. Government Printing Office, 1993.

_____. *What Work Requires of Schools.* Washington: U.S. Government Printing Office, 1991.

Whitehead, Alfred North. *Process and Reality.* New York: Free Press, 1979.